Reflections

Reflections

John Woolslair Sheppard

With writings by
Mary Woolslair Sheppard
and
Harriet McCoy Woolslair

Strathmoor Books

Manufactured in the United States of America

Library of Congress Control Number: 133483

ISBN: 1-881539-26-1

Book design and production: Tabby House

Cover design: Pearl & Associates

Strathmoor Books

4429 Shady Lane

Charlotte Harbor, FL 33980

Dedication

To my best friend, my wife Ellen; to my greatest gifts in life, my children Andy and Sandy; to their spouses Carolyn and Carl; to my greatest joys in life, my grandchildren Erik, Carl, Brett, Lauren Elyse and Johnny B.; and above all, to the One who gives, sustains and gives meaning to life.

"As a face is reflected in water so the heart reflects the person."
Proverbs 27:19 (NLB) King Solomon

Contents

Acknowledgments   *xi*

Preface   *xii*

Part I   Reflections on Life   1

Part II   Personal Reflections   113

Part III   Reflections of My Heritage   147

Index, by Title   165

Acknowledgments

I thank my wife, Ellen, for her encouragement and support in all things, for her reading and listening, and helpful suggestions. To my friend and client of thirty years, George Sanders, thanks for his inspiration on living life, and for our early morning conversations about faith and family. And to my aunt, Ethlyn Sheppard Cheney, ninety-seven. I have learned much from her during the past thirty years about the importance of forthrightness, love, and having the right attitude.

And, finally, I thank my father, W. A. Sheppard, who died in 1971. He was the most principled man I have every known. He was not only my father, but my partner, my mentor, my teacher and my friend. He was also a father figure to Ellen. I respected him more than any man. I shall always treasure the twelve years I was privileged to work with him. It was he who taught me the value of hard work—that one's integrity must remain inviolate; that loyalty and commitment to those we serve and love must never be compromised; that there must be sanctity of information given to me in confidence, and that one's word must be his bond. And, that these things are to be treasured above all the status and riches of the world. I am thankful for his lessons in life.

Preface

Years ago my mother gave me a short poem that my grandmother had written titled "Courage." It is a powerful poem about standing in the storms of life. My wife, Ellen, was so taken with it that she placed it at eye height on a cabinet in our kitchen. How many times we both have read its words again and again and, they have given us strength in life's storms. When my mother died in 1998, I found among her belongings a series of poems that my grandmother had written, all of which are included in this volume, as well as one that was in my mother's handwriting.

Reading their poems inspired me to put in verse form some of my thoughts and reflections. I had only written verse several times through the years, reflecting on important events in life.

But now I am sixty-eight years old. So, is the cup half filled or half empty? It is a question of attitude and perspective. Either way, it's more like ninety-five percent. Realizing my mortality, I began to look back over my life—what I've observed, some things I have learned, some truths I have discovered. I wanted to express some of these thoughts and observations, with the hope that they might help someone who is traveling along life's way.

It occurred to me that verse might be a good way to express these ideas and concepts so I began to study its different forms. I settled on the couplet form because of its simplicity. In several writings I have used the anaphora form primarily for emphasis of a key word or idea, and in at least one, have combined it with the couplet form.

Part One contains reflections about life. Part Two contains personal reflections, with some vignettes of my family's life. Part Three contains writings of my grandmother Harriet McCoy Woolslair and my mother Mary Woolslair Sheppard. One of my grandmother's poems, "In our Backyard," speaks of her home and life in the early part of the twentieth century. I have included my writing by the same title, which reflects upon my own family's backyard some sixty years later.

You will find that there is an introduction to each of the poems in Part One and Two, to provide background. Most of the poems in the second section are light and can be read in a wisp, while Part Three reflect my grandmother's faith and her life.

In his trial before Pontius Pilate, Jesus of Nazareth, proclaimed that He had "come to bear witness to the Truth." Pilate responded with the question "What is truth?" (John 18: 37–38) Jesus had said earlier, "You shall know the Truth and the Truth shall set you free." (John 8: 32) I believe that truth is in life—we just have to find it, and know what it is, when we find it.

I am searching every day for truth in life. What I have tried to do in these writings is to express certain "truths" I have found. Some are in scripture, others in life experiences, and others in observing the passing parade of life. We will never know all of truth on this side of "the river." We only have glimpses of it. As the Apostle Paul said, "Now we see in the mirror but dimly, but then face to face, now I know in part, but then I shall I shall know fully, just as I am fully known." (1 Corinthians 13:12)

It is my hope then that you might get just a glimpse of some truth in these verses, and at the very least, that it might encourage you to search further for it, as it is, and will be revealed to you.

Part One
Reflections on Life

My Advocate

James D. "Jim" and Ellie Newton have been friends of mine for more than thirty years. I met Jim through my work when he came to my office with Leonardo Santini, an elderly client of mine, to discuss a business matter. Leonardo, seventy-eight years old, was a gracious and generous man. And as his friend and counselor, I felt very protective of him. Jim Newton had just retired from service with Moral Rearmament and started a new real estate business at age sixty-seven. The proposal that day was to build a 181-unit condominium—a new concept of construction in Florida in the early 1970s—on a part of Mr. Santini's beach property. It was to be the largest condominium project ever done in the county at that time.

My first reaction was to think how do I get this "old guy," Jim, out of Leonardo's life? Why did Leonardo, a widowed, retired farmer and fisherman, need to go into a condominium project and finance it through a bank, with a sixty-seven-year-old new real estate broker to oversee it? But, after listening to Jim for thirty minutes, not only was I sold on the idea, I was enthusiastic about it. Though I thought I was a pretty hard nut to crack—I had heard it all— I was sold on the deal, but more sold on the man. As it turned out, the project was extremely successful and the pair went on to build a shopping center. It was the greatest thing to happen in Leonardo's remaining life. Not only did his new interests give him longevity, it gave him some wonderful new friends, and enabled him to substantially increase his wealth—in which he has left a wonderful charitable and religious legacy to the community for generations to come in perpetuity.

Jim and I became not just working friends, but soul mates, as we shared our faith and our lives over the next three decades.

In 1987 Jim wrote a bestselling book titled *Uncommon Friends* about his friendship with Thomas Edison, Henry Ford, Harvey Firestone,

Alexis Correll and Charles Lindberg. The story behind the book was made into a documentary and presented on PBS in 2000.

In late 1998, Jim and I began to talk frequently about his "graduation" to the next life because his health was poor. We had talked about "graduation" for years and about "the best is yet to come," but it had always been in the future. But now, we both knew, the time was near.

In early October, a few months before his death in December 1999, Jim expressed concern to me about his "future." He realized that he had imperfections in life—though they were not perceptible to others. I told him that if he didn't make the Promised Land, probably none of us would. That beyond that we are all imperfect, that this is what Grace is all about.

I told Jim that while I had tried to be his counselor and friend, he had a real Advocate in Jesus. He said "What do you mean?" I said it's right in the Scripture in 1 John 2, 1–2: "My little children, if anyone falls short, We have an Advocate with the Father, Jesus the Righteous." Jim said he'd never heard of that idea. We talked about it at some length, and it seemed to give him a peace about things.

Several days later, I sat down at my desk, and the words of "My Advocate" came out and gave a copy to Jim. Later, when he was ill, I took a framed copy to him and discovered that he had already framed a copy. Jim, Ellie and I sat in his bedroom, and he said, "One will be mine, the other for Ellie." He placed his next to his bed on a little table, below a painting of "The High Priest." Jim asked that I read "The Advocate" at his graduation ceremony, which I gladly did.

I wrote this for my dear friend Jim Newton. I hope that it might comfort for others who begin thinking about their own mortality and imperfections, and how fortunate we are to have One who knows our every thought, and who will speak for us at our graduation, if we will but take Him into our life, call Him friend, and acknowledge Him as the One who can make right all of our failures in life.

My Advocate

In God's own time, there shall come a day
When I shall have finally passed this way
And I shall stand at the bar of His great throne
Before I go, to my eternal home.

On that great day, He shall judge my life
Which has seen both beauty, failure and strife.
And, then, I shall see my life past, so clearly
What I had seen before, only in a mirror dimly.

And while I know I should stand in trembling and fear
With the mighty power of my God so near.
But I shall fear no more, because of Jesus' grace
When I shall meet my Master, face to face.

For Jesus gave His life, His very blood
That I might stand amidst life's raging flood,
And on that day, all my sins are laid to rest
By His blood and life, I have passed the test.

Oh what a comfort it is to me
To know when I pass o'er the Crystal Sea
That standing by me in that judgment time
Is Jesus, my Advocate, I, the lost one, of the ninety and nine.

For He is greater than all the prophets of old
Greater than all the angels, playing their harps of gold
Greater than a thousand Jennings Bryans and Clarence Darrows
Jesus, my Advocate, my defender, my bow and my arrow.

For when the Book is opened and I am asked, "Why?"
It shall be Jesus, the Righteous, who speaks for me, not I
And He shall say, "Though he often failed, he earnestly tried,
It was for his failures, that I willingly died."

"And though he stumbled day by day
He tried as you asked, to show kindness and justice, along the way.
And even as he faltered, he sought to walk with His God
On all the paths and pilgrimage, that he has trod."

And, so it is armed with this blessed assurance
That I need not fear, when I give up my last, my endurance
For Jesus, my rock, my Advocate, my defender
Shall take me home, to that eternal place of splendor.

Scriptural references: 1 John 2: 1–2 "My little children ...if anyone sins, We have an Advocate with the Father, Jesus the Righteous." (RSV, NAS)
Micah 6: 8; Matthew 18: 10–14; 1 Corinthians 13: 12; Revelation 20: 11–15.

Like a Two-edged Sword

A former client of mine called me the other day. Although I tried to fake it, at first I really didn't remember him by name. Once we began talking, however, I remembered him well. He was a pleasant and thoughtful elderly gentleman. He asked me for a reference on some changes he wanted to make on his life plan. He said he remembered well what I had told him fifteen years ago that, among other things, the purpose in life was to do justice to others, to show mercy, and to walk humbly with your God. (I have to admit, it wasn't my thought, but the words of the prophet Micah in the Old Testament.) Anyway, he went on to say that he counted me among five men in his life who had had the most impact on his life. Wow! That was both awesome and scary, especially since he was a man I only knew professionally. I had no recollection of what I had said to him or when it was said, and yet it had a significant impact on his life. I recalled another man who had come to my office several years ago and said that the advice I had given him twenty years earlier had been the guiding principle of his financial and family plans for the next two decades. Everything had worked out perfectly. But suppose I had been careless, uncaring or not thorough in what my advice had been? The wrong could have negatively affected his life and that of his family.

Truly the words that come from our mouths can change lives for good or bad. And sometimes we hurt others and don't even know it. How important it is that we carefully consider what we say. Sometimes our words can be literally an issue of life or death.

Like a Two-edged Sword

The most powerful organ within each of us, ounce for ounce,
The one that gives our personality a hefty bounce,
Is that two-ounce monster lying in wait, within our mouth.
The tongue, like a ship's rudder, sends us on a course, either
      north or south.

God planted the tongue behind the cage of our teeth
To keep it in check, to only carefully, take this sword from its sheath.
For the tongue, though small, has awesome destructive power
With one blow, it can bring down the mighty, turn a whole life
      sour.

Or it can just rattle on, just to be talking, is so much palaver.
'Tis wasted energy, misuses God's gift, just to use it for jabber.
Sometimes the talk is empty, just so much wind
With no real purpose, no message to send.

The tongue like so many things was not created to do bad
Even though we use it, all too often, when we become mad.
Yet it can be used not only to destroy, but to do great good
If only it's great power were completely understood.

For the words we speak are as arrows from a cross and bow.
Sometimes thoughtless shots can injure or destroy, more than we
      know.
And yet the same tongue, can with words, that are like a skillful
      surgeon's knife
Heal a wound, excise an emotional tumor, or even save a desperate
      life.

There are then, things about the tongue, and its words, we need to
      comprehend
That the words we speak, may, know it or not, create an enemy, or
      win a friend.
Yet the tongue should not be condemned, for it is simply the messenger
Of an angry, hurt or malicious heart, that is striking out, to
      create a stir.

The very same heart may with words, give compassion, build up,
      encourage or heal.
Can change or set new direction for a young life, or renew an older
      one to feel
That their very existence is important, a life to be treasured and
      prized.
With words that calm fears, create new horizons, in ways, that leave
      even the speaker surprised.

Our words are like a two-edged sword, one edge pierces deeply,
      the other restores.
One edge affirms, the other batters, one edge brings joy, the other
      remorse.
Carefully choose then, and carefully speak, the right words for the
      occasion
That your words might lift another up, or bring friendly persuasion.

Sometimes our most effective words may be no words at all.
Just our very presence may speak volumes, and tragedy forestall,
Using words then as our tools, our excellent instruments of healing.
Choose them selectively, just the right implement, for the
      circumstance we're dealing.

Because our spoken words have the power to create or destroy
We need to carefully consider, when and how our words to deploy.
Our words need to be thoughtfully molded and carefully conceived
For their impact on others may go far beyond, what we could have
      believed.

The Times of Our Life

Anyone who is a student of the Old Testament, and particularly the Book of Ecclesiastes, may recognize the same ideas expressed in a song performed by the BYRDS—a popular musical group in the 1960s and early 1970s. The song, called "Turn, Turn, Turn," tracks chapter 3, verses 1–7 of Ecclesiastes as it looks at the extremes of life (the turns). Solomon described life by saying as "all is vanity." Life itself, he said in Ecclesiastes, is a series of ups and down, ins and outs. There is then a time for everything. For everything there is a season. "The Times of Our Life" picks up on this idea, and says we will experience all of these things.

What is important is first to recognize "what time it is" and to deal with that particular time in our life wisely. And whatever time it may be in our life, we must live it out, as best we can, to enjoy the good times, and to learn from the difficult ones. And as we do, we should remember that better things are to come. Solomon, who is said to be the wisest man who ever lived, observed that all of the "stuff" that we pursue in life is vanity. And, after twelve chapters, concludes that the most important thing we can do in our life is to put God first. Think about it.

The Times of Our Life

Life looked at through the microscope of day to day
May seem to you, either out of control, or a boring picture portray.
Yet, if we were able to stand back, and see our life as a whole
'Tis a passing parade, swinging between ennui and ecstasy,
      mountain and pothole.

So while life may appear to you, either a difficult journey, or an
      endless plain
That the challenge of exciting things happen to others, for us it is
      just the mundane.
Into each life, at some time, both rain and sunshine shall surely
      send.
Life has storms and calm, it's not a question of whether,
      but of how and when.

So, it is with the times of our life, there is a time for everything
There is a time for work and a time to recreate, a time to hum,
      and time to sing
There is a time for precision, and a time to be loose.
There is a time for explanation, and a time for no excuse.

There is a time to eat, and a time to fast.
There is a time to give away, and a time to amass.
There is a time to be angry, and a time to forgive.
There is a time to exist, and a time to live.

There is a time to be silent, and a time to speak.
There is a time to be bold, and a time to be meek.
There is a time to push away, and a time to embrace.
There is a time to strike out anew, and time to retrace.

There is a time to look, and a time to turn away.
There is a time to question, and a time to pray.
There is a time to be certain, and a time to have doubt.

There is a time to speak softly, and a time to shout.
There is a time to climb mountains, and a time to descend.
There is a time to be independent, and a time to depend.
There is a time of plenty, and a time of need.
There is a time to root up, and a time to seed.

There is a time to love, and a time to hate.
There is a time to stand up, and a time to prostrate.
There is a time to hold on to, and a time to release.
There is a time for our wars and a time for our peace.

There is a time to contest, and a time to accept.
There is a time to let pass, and a time to intercept.
There is a time to laugh, and a time to cry.
There is time to be born, and a time to die.

And though most of life is spent between these extremes
There are daily swings of the pendulum, through
        which we find what life means.
Because it is often in the times of trial and stress,
        that we grow the most
That we learn the important lessons of life,
        that will be our guide posts.

The test of our learning and wisdom, then is to know what time,
        for us, it is
That we take each time of our life, live it fully, with nothing to miss.
And knowing what time it is, that we appropriately respond
Knowing that others through time, have been where we are since
        man's life first dawned.

As we look at our life then, and see each day as much the same,
May we realize there are daily swings and challenges that a life will
        claim.
May we be thankful for the times of joy, and learn in the times of
        sorrow
With the assurance, that better things are coming, in God's time, on
        His Tomorrow.

The Why Questions of Life

When we were in grammar school years ago, our English teacher taught us that an adverb is a word or phrase that modifies, explains or expands upon a verb. The adverbial phrase answers the questions of who, what, when, where and why. Life itself has a lot of "adverbial" questions. The who, what, when, and where questions we can usually figure out, either by observation, experience, knowledge or wisdom. It is the "why" questions that often confound us. The "why" questions don't always add up from what we know, observe, or experience. Two and two don't always equal four. Life is not always fair.

Recently I was asked to speak at the dedication of a memorial site at a children's cancer center, remembering children who had died of cancer. I looked out over some of the fifty family members gathered, all of whom had lost children, and tried to bring them a message of hope, coming from the depth of their loss. What I saw before me was a sea of tears. Again I asked the unanswerable question of why these children had died. Not how, when or where questions, but why did they have to die? Why not me, or someone else instead of them?

I concluded long ago, as I had wrestled with these questions in my own life experience, that I do not have the answer to the question. I defy anyone to give a rational answer that makes sense—and adds up—in human terms. And, I have found that patronizing or glib answers only exacerbate a painful situation and confuse those who are grieving.

The answers that I have found are from the promises of scripture. It is to acknowledge that life isn't always fair, even when we give ourselves unconditionally in love. Pain and hurt come to all of us, whether we are good or bad, they are a part of the cycle of love and life. But I have also found that faith can give us peace, and the ability to work through the difficult times, and the hope and assurance that life does not end on this earth. And further, that not only is their something

13

beyond this earth, but we will have the answers to all of the "why" questions of this life, which will be then understood beyond human terms, but in eternal terms. In this world the things that will sustain us through good and bad times are faith, hope and love, and the greatest of these is love—unconditional love, even though we risk the pain of loss. It is more than worth the risk.

The Why Questions of Life

There are ponderous mysteries of life and nature,
     we don't understand.
Questions about the universe's creation, solar systems,
     remote wastelands.
And the mystery of life, from two cells to completion
     of a human being
Through science, we see a fetus develop, not comprehending
     what we're seeing.

Even evolution and creation, which are the subjects of much debate
We can't logically prove either, that would to the others' advocates,
     accommodate.
Even the so called laws of gravity, we know exist, but don't know why
Or how or why there are thousands of solar systems in the sky.

Why is it then, with all of the enigmas of nature, we can't explain
That we become bewildered, when answers to life's travails,
     we seek in vain.
There are things that happen in our lives and those we love,
     without explanation
That we have no more understanding of, than the exegesis
     of all creation.

For even if we explored a lifetime, or researched endlessly
     at a school or college,
There are things, man was told, that are forbidden fruit of the
     tree of knowledge.
And similarly, we can search forever, seeking answers to life's events
Those inexplicable things that happen, that we'd most like
     to prevent.

Questions about why children and young people die before their time
The lost life, not lived out, the pain and grief left behind.
Or why one child is born disabled, while another is born whole?
To say Providence had a reason, with parent's grief and guilt,
       does not console.

And why does evil seem to prosper, while the righteous suffer
Why some seem to have it so easy, while others' struggles
       are much rougher?
But, we were never promised ease in life, rain falls on the
       good and bad alike.
The promise is, that in His own time, He will make things right.

How, then, are we to make sense of these things,
       that defy human reason?
We must reconcile that the joy and hurt of life, each will have
       its own season.
And that even out of the pains of life, we can seek and find our peace
Even when we cannot change what has happened,
       there can be release.
If this be true, then, that our faith offers us no protective shield.
Then what does it offer us, that in our time of hurt,
       we might be healed.
It is the promise that the end of this life, is not the end
       of our existence
That we walk not alone, we shall have all answers one day,
       at His insistence.

And, if we will but wait—
There shall come a time, when we shall gain new strength
       and not grow weary.
And there shall come a time when we shall know real peace,
       not just man's theory.
And there shall come a time when the broken bodies and hearts
       are healed,
And there shall come a time when all our unresolved questions
       are revealed.

Scriptural references: Genesis 3: 1–3; Ecclesiastes 3: 18; Psalm 73; Isaiah 11: 6;
Isaiah 40: 28–31; Matthew 6: 45; John 9: 1–5; 1 Corinthians 13, 12;
1 Corinthians 15: 35–44.

The Blessing

The story of Esau, brother of Jacob and son of Isaac, that appears in the Old Testament Book of Genesis, is a tragic one. Esau, who we gather from the story is the older of twin brothers, a man of great physical strength, a hard worker, but lacked the mental agility of his younger brother, Jacob. Under early Jewish law, which was carried down to the common law of England, the rule of primogeniture applied—the oldest son, upon death of the father, became head of the family. The oldest son essentially owned and controlled the property and family of the father. This then was Esau's right and inheritance.

As the story goes, Esau, in a fit of hunger, traded his inheritance to Jacob for a bowl of stew. Jacob then tricked his father, Isaac, into giving him the "blessing" normally given to the elder son. The term "blessing" still has special significance to the Jewish people. However, the concept of giving our children "blessing" or "affirmation" is as critical to the child's well being, as is feeding and nurturing.

Because Isaac blessed Jacob first, even though he was tricked into it, he refused to give Esau a "blessing" of any kind.

Psychologists today would tell us that many children who have never received the approval or "blessing" of their parents, whether consciously or unconsciously withheld, carry that burden with them throughout life. The blessing, then, is about the need of each of us to have approval and affirmation, not only by our parents but others as well. One of the greatest gifts we can give to each other is the gift of affirmation, if not of a particular action, at least affirmation and blessing of others as individuals.

The Blessing

Four thousand years ago, there was a man named Esau
The son of Isaac, a strong and burly man,
    who'd something in his craw.
For his younger brother Jacob,
    whom his mom had always loved the best
Had tricked his dad, Isaac, took Esau's inheritance,
    and bequest.

Not only that, but Jacob tricked his blind father
    and got Esau's blessing
He put on his brother's clothes, cooked Dad a meal,
    never his deceit confessing.
Yet what hurt Esau the most,
    was not the loss of the land of his inheritance
But that his father would not bless or affirm him,
    under any circumstance.

The pain of his father's rejection followed Esau all of his life.
He lived as a man of anger, his mind and heart filled with strife
Until one day, years later perchance, would Esau and Jacob meet
Jacob was contrite, sorrowed at what he'd done, fell at Esau's feet.

Only then, did Esau's early rejection and life of pain, begin to heal
His father's blessing and approval withheld, the love
    he needed to feel
If only Esau's father, would have given him the affirmation
    he refused to say
To tell his son Esau he loved him, his life had great value,
    and said "You're OK."

May we then learn lessons from this ancient story of long ago.
There is one thing that each child, yea each person, needs to know
That we are each God's unique creation, like no other, special to Him
We need to be affirmed by someone, whose cup of love,
    is filled to the brim.

Our need for approbation begins with
     an inner need to please our parents
And for parents to withhold that approval,
     plants bitter seeds to ferment.
But that need to have another's blessing,
     extends far beyond the home
For we need the assurance of family,
     workers and friends, to know we're not alone.

Each of us then has a lifelong need from the date of our birth
To know that we, among all, are a creature of great worth.
We need to affirm those around us, that they may know
That they too are unique and special, a blessing on them to bestow.

A priceless gem that we each own, and may give or receive
Is an unconditional blessing, telling another that in him we believe.
And out of our blessing, surely many great things will flow
For it gives life meaning, and assurance,
     it is the leaven for the dough.

The Voyage

Some time ago, I was asked to do a eulogy at the funeral of a lifelong friend. As I began to think about his life, and about his passage through this life and into the next life, thoughts and ideas began to surface about the analogy of sailing, even beyond the horizon. The idea of "sailing" to the other side is not a new one. Longfellow perhaps said it best in his "Crossing the Bar." I have tried to expand on the idea, that the passage is not to be feared, but more to be looked on as a new unknown adventure. Certainly death is something that we'd rather "put off until tomorrow." On the other hand, we should regard it with anticipation, as a passage from one life into the next. The comparison has been made between death and the afterlife and the incubation and growth of a child in the mother's womb, followed by birth. Death is a new beginning—a new birth. I am comforted by the knowledge and belief of my faith, that while I really don't know what lies on the other side, I have assurance that I need have no fear of it. As the Apostle Paul said in Philippians 4: 13, "I can do and endure all things through Christ who strengthens me."

The Voyage

Some time, some day, I'm not certain when
I shall loose my moorings and sail away.
Maybe slowly, maybe suddenly, without farewell, or note penned
To my friends, and ones I've loved, who are anchored on my bay.

Silently, then I shall ease away
Just as night slips in at the close of day.
And as the skiffs anchored 'round me move to and fro,
Some time some day, I don't know, when my wind shall blow.
But on that day, I shall, without fear,
⠀⠀⠀⠀⠀sail beyond the horizon of our vision
On a new voyage, that we don't know,
⠀⠀⠀⠀⠀to a new destination and dimension.

There will be some who have known me, who will feel dismay
And will miss my vessel on our special bay.
Some whose schooners have been anchored near
Some who loved me, were close to me, for many years
Will grieve my passage, and shed their tears.

But, I shall have set course on a new adventure
To a new safe harbor sheltered from the storm, and secure.
And I shall dock with ones I knew, who have sailed this course before
Beyond the horizon, to the unseen distant sea, to my Captain's
⠀⠀⠀⠀⠀peaceful shore.

For I know that He has prepared a special place for me
A quiet haven at water's edge, of His beautiful Crystal Sea
And, I shall dock my ship with Him for eternity
And await those loved ones who had grieved for me.
For they, too, shall some day, loose their moorings and sail away
Then, we shall all be together, with our Captain, forever and a day.

The Eagle Has Landed

For years I have been an early morning runner, beginning shortly after dawn on Saturday mornings.

Several years ago I was running on an asphalt road near my home, when I came upon a large bird working on "road kill." At first I was sure it was a hawk, or maybe a buzzard, but as I came closer, I realized it was a rare bald eagle, still on the endangered species list. I stopped, shocked, yet in awe of this might bird. I had only seen a few bald eagles before, always from the distance, always majestically and gracefully gliding in the upper winds. Yet here he was—proud and brave warrior in earlier years—now on the surface of the road, limping and gimping around, as a crippled ineffective animal. Is he, like we Americans, once free and independent, now bound by our rules and regulations, and completely interdependent?

The Eagle has Landed

I had ventured out at dawn for my early morning run
Spotted a majestic bird, in the distant air, as I'd just begun
Often before, I'd see large birds, hoping it'd be an eagle,
    the great bird
Only to realize, that it was a vulture, or a brown hawk,
    no emotion stirred.

I thought how despicable, was the vulture, the relentless scavenger
Though useful, living off of death, and leftovers
    of another animal hunter.
Even the hawk, steals the eggs and baby chicks,
    of many smaller birds
Chased off by the relentless tiny mocking birds,
    David and Goliath, seems absurd.

But as I watched carefully, as the large bird glided ever closer to me
It really was an enormous bald eagle, so rare and exciting to see.
He sailed through the air with grace, the wind beneath his wings
Diving and climbing, turning his pure white head,
    a resplendent thing.

I changed my running direction, just to follow his course
As he scoured the area, for some wild animal, to strike with force
I thought here is a creature, wonderfully made,
    respected, even revered
The king of all birds, strong beak and talons,
    magnificently engineered.

And then suddenly, as I ran down the road following him.
He swooped down, I was sure some creature, to meet his requiem
To my surprise, this noble animal, landed on the road,
    just yards from me.
I stopped short to watch, surely he'd fly off,
    talons clutching his abductee.

23

As I watched, he limped on his talons, as a cripple,
        on the surface of the road
There was no live game he had hunted, to take back
        to waiting mouths at his abode.
But rather a luckless raccoon, struck by a car, would be his meal
My visions of this revered mystical creature shattered,
        seemed surreal.

Had he, the symbol of America, home of the brave and the free
Become, in our sprawling society, by necessity,
        a scavenger, a tragedy to see?
Or was this just an aberration, not a change of his life in ages past
Would this strong proud creature, stay true to his heritage,
        to the last?

As I've thought about that early morning,
        when the soaring eagle landed
I was disillusioned by what I saw,
        his weakness and frailty, to be candid.
But then I realized that he like all of God's creatures,
        women and men,
Are frail and imperfect, and we await that time,
        when He will make us perfect again.

Pearls of Life

There is a parable that appears in Matthew 13:45-46—the parable of
the hidden treasure. It reads: "Again the Kingdom of Heaven is like the
merchant seeking fine pearls, and upon finding one pearl of great value,
he went and sold all that he had and bought it." While the parable has
multiple meanings for Christians, I began to think about the analogy
of pearls and life, and finding wisdom and truth in life as I was reading
that parable some time ago. I began to think about how natural pearls
are formed from irritant grains of sand. And yet from that irritant to
the oyster shell comes beautiful, valuable gems, and how they are hid-
den beneath the sea, and how we must search for them. I saw parallels
between pearls and meanings in life itself, and from there, how a string
of varied pearls of all kinds, likewise paralleled life itself. In a sense,
we are all searching for the pearls of life that give us truth, wisdom,
satisfaction, and peace. The same Gospel of Matthew 8:32, tells us that
"You shall know the Truth, and the Truth shall set you free." What a
great promise!

Pearls of Life

The pearl is a creation of rare beauty, a treasure that is sought.
For thousands of years men have desired it, at great price bought.
Yet the pearl is small, its appearance not bright, as other gems.
Men have searched far and wide, for the perfect pearl,
      the crème de la crème.

And yet the pure pearl is only found in the faraway depths of the sea.
So man does search it out, sometimes at risk of his life, to set it free.
The little pearl, which begins with a grain of sand, an irritation,
      within a shell.
Sheltered, as is a grain of truth in the mind of man, growing in
      beauty, as it inward dwells.

So, as with the pearl, are the treasures of truth of life all around
Beginning as a thought, imperceptibly growing in beauty, to abound.
As with the pearl, life's treasures must be found, and are beyond our
      vision.
Often, the task is long, requires commitment, and has no precision.

But once one of these pearls of life, we have come to know.
We want to hold it, possess it, and never let it go.
The pearls of life, of love, and wisdom, though, are things we need to
      share
For these are jewels we have just discovered, do not own, for they
      have always been there.

Life pearls of great worth, truth has both outer and inner beauty.
To study each found pearl, to test its mettle, our solemn duty.
For we must find that these pearls of truth, we hold cradled in our
      hand
Will stand the test of time and truth, that which was once as a grain
      of sand.

And if the natural pearl is artificial, not pure or true, that too will
     surface,
Just as will insincerity, hypocrisy, dishonesty, or ulterior purpose.
And all the pearls, which we find, and which cross our path
Will not have value, and some spawn negative results and wrath.

Even true pearls which are drawn from undersea do not bring the
     same price.
There value is measured by shape, size, color and clarity
     to be concise.
So, too, with the pearls of life, though they may be true,
     the valued pearls are only rare.
It is those rare pearls we need to seek out, to hold onto,
     yet nurture and share.

Similarly, a string of pearls of many different shades and colors are
     like life's days
And the string that holds the pearls together, is as the thread of life,
     and its many ways.
Every day, like every pearl, is different, some black, some white,
     some cloudy, some pure.
Each day a gift, and we often don't know which kind of pearl a day
     will be, for sure.

Some days, as some pearls, will have far greater value in the sum of
     our life.
Some days will be as white or blue-hued pearls, beautiful
     and pleasant, without strife.
Other days, as a cloudy pearl, will seem bland and valueless
     or leave us in doubt
And there will black days of pain, but as rare black pearls,
     priceless to teach us what life's about.

And the strong clasp that holds the string of varied pearls together
That gives our life's voyage meaning and direction,
     whatever be the weather.
It is that each of us is God's unique creation,
     sojourners placed here for just a time.
That we might leave a gift, by example set, a heritage,
     a legacy for all mankind.

So what are those valued pearls, that are for you,
    and which you should seek to find.
Each person must make his own search and journey,
    with his heart, his spirit and mind.
But as for me, in my life's pilgrimage,
    among the most worthy pearls I have found
Are God, Love, Integrity, Justice, Compassion, Mercy,
    Forgiveness, and Humility to be crowned.

Forgive and Let Go

"Forgive and Let Go" is about finding the right time to let go of past hurts and wrongs that have been done to us. It is about making a conscious effort to forgive those who have either consciously or unknowingly caused us pain. Even when forgiveness is sometimes not possible, in its most complete sense, such as when the person rejects your forgiveness, has died, or is unavailable, there is a time to let go.

John Woolslair Sheppard

Forgive and Let Go

One of the most difficult things you have to do
Is to forgive the person who has deeply offended you.
Maybe they spoke something of you, that was entirely wrong
Or betrayed a confidence shared with them, far too long.

Sometimes the offense might seem to others, such a little thing
Treating you as inferior, a lesser person, or an underling.
It may have been a love lost, you thought would never end
And they deserted you, and in the pits, did you descend.

Sometimes we're hurt by others, things done or said,
        they don't even know
We couldn't say anything at the time, and let our feelings show
So we buried it deep within our psyche, the offense committed
Only to dig it up again and again,
        rehearsing our lines, to be quick-witted.

Or maybe it was abusive treatment we survived as a child
The scars and the pain still there, the way we were reviled.
For some it was a harsh or destructive words spoken, never retracted
These things have stayed with us these years, their toll extracted.

There are so many ways by which we inflict pain
On one another, leaving on our hearts an indelible stain.
But there comes a time when we must open up,
        and deal with these things
That hurt us to the core, our anger and bitterness,
        they continue to bring.

Our wounds and pains come in all shapes, sizes and dimensions
But harbored within us, overtime, create ever-growing tensions
Somehow we need to resolve them, to get them fully out
Whether it be by sharing with others, writing it down,
        or a plaintive shout.

The best way to let the pain and anguish of our past go
Is to confront the offender, to let them really know.
Yet we know 'tis not possible to do in all situations
To discuss and resolve your hurt, and restore the relation.

And even where a new dialogue does occur, for reasons whatever
It may fail to resolve the pain, in spite of your endeavor.
But, you need to give resolution and forgiveness, your very best
So that, resolved or not, you may put this past to rest.

For sometimes the person who brought on your grief
Will acknowledge no fault, blaming you, which brings no relief.
If this happens, and you've tried the best that you could
And your effort has been rejected, your effort misunderstood.

At this point, you need to examine the lasting hurt that's been done
And know that harboring anger and resentment, will hurt only one.
The time then has come, you must let it all go, you see
For only when you have released it, will you finally be free.

The Wave

Some fifty years ago, I wrote a three-line poem titled "The Wave" for a high school English class. The poem read, "Each wave rolls stealthily in, sprawls upon the shore, / Slips quickly out to sea again, / To be seen no more." Fifty years later I wrote another poem called "The Wave." Neither is very profound, but the second takes the first's idea but a different approach—the parallel between a wave being a part of the ocean, and our life as being a part of all mankind, and the larger universe.

The Wave

I sit with bended knees on the sandy shore,
Looking seaward and reflecting quietly on the days of yore.
And I think of the days that for me are yet to come
These days of life, moving so swiftly, like the racer's run.

Each wave is born far out at sea
Far beyond the point my eyes can see.
And as the waves move in, becoming ever more strong
Singing quietly their rippling, constant song.

As I watch the waves moving methodically in
And wonder where did each its own journey begin.
Each wave is unique, as the sun glistens through
In a sense like us, for each of us is so different, too.

I pick my wave to watch, as it continues to roll
And, wonder if even it too, might have a soul.
Then suddenly it begins to foam and crest
Followed quickly by another, nearly coming abreast.

Then as my wave finally nears the shore,
It moves closer quickly, its strength bristling to the core,
Splashes upon the beach with a mighty roar.
Its spirit, then slips quietly out to sea, to its source—
To be seen no more.

Manly Tears

Tears are a part of our lives, from the moment of birth until the last breath of life. Tears flow freely for many reasons when we are young. As we grow older, especially for we males, tears are suppressed—they aren't considered manly or appropriate. Science has discovered that tears release healing endorphins. Tears express a great range of emotion from pain to fear, to relief to joy. "Tears" expresses the importance of honoring tears as a needed part and expression at significant times in our life.

Manly Tears

The tears of the infant come with a shrieking cry
The anxious parent seeks desperately to know why.
They may be tears of pain, hunger, or need of a touch
Or they may be tears of distress and such.

The tears of the young child come often, to express many emotions
Of anger, frustration, a skinned knee, and need of a notion.
But they come freely to express whatever he feels,
These tears that express the moments of his ordeals.

But as he grows older, he learns not to cry.
It is not good, nor manly, to express your feelings, that's why.
We are taught that a real man should never show his tears
'Tis better to deny our emotions, our pain, joy and fears.

And as we grow to manhood, then, we've learned to bury within
Keep it all inside, let no one know, let no one in.
And the pain of insecurity, rejection, failures, from broken relations
Keep it inside, share with no one, show outward calm and patience.

And I think, surely I'm the only one who hurts and feels this way
No one else has these hurts and feelings, that we can't display.
If only there was someone who would listen, and really hear
If only I could feel whole in releasing these tears.

Somehow we must recycle these lessons we're taught
To know that the pain we've held within, what it's wrought.
That God gave each of us emotions that we need to express
That our deepest joys, our fears, our pains might be addressed.

For we need to know that when one is troubled, his eyes aglisten
There is need for release, there is need of a friend to listen.
To bury, to deny, to conceal the emotions we feel
Is to make us unhappy, confuse us, to deny what is real.

35

But as I've grown older, through the years I've known
In my life seeds of love, joy, pain and failure have been sewn.
I've come to know that in my tears shed, there is no shame
Rather than weakness, my tears reflect an inner strength to remain.

For it is in our touch and our tears, we show that we care.
Tears of joy, tears of grief, tears of love, that we share
The outward expression of love and compassion, can't be wrong.
Rather than weakness, they reflect our commitment is strong.

If only this truth could be learned early in our years
That in times of great love, grief, pain and joy, we can shed our tears.
For these are but a part of our whole being, our true humanity
And to deny, or repress them, is to show only our vanity.

Why 2 K

On New Year's Eve 1999, for the first time in many years, I stayed up until midnight to see in the new millennium. I thoroughly enjoyed the television coverage of the New Year's celebrations, and was pleasantly surprised, despite widespread concerns, that the world neither exploded nor imploded. Maybe, just maybe, the dire predictions of doom will be like Mark Twain's statement as to rumors of his death—"slightly exaggerated." Maybe, even with the beginning of a new millennium, there is some hope for this old world. As one person said, there really is nothing new or different in the world, just new people finding new ways to make the same old mistakes.

Why 2 K

As I awoke early this morning, I was thankful for a beautiful day
Though early awakenings are daily events at my ancient age
But there was something very special about this glorious day
The beginning of a new century, a new millennium, on the way.

I leaped out of bed, and rushed to the window, to see
If the world was still there, then cut on the TV.
I was so excited, concerned, nearly lost my breath
With predictions of catastrophic failures, violence and death.

And to my surprise and delight, I viewed that all was well
The cynical had warned of atomic blasts, societal collapse,
          a death knell.
But to the contrary, everything seemed quite the same
Our earth, the country, our town had survived, would still remain.

I had watched the celebrations on the evening before:
Fireworks, happy revelers o'er the world, from shore to shore.
How happy I was, the transition so smooth, without mystery
On this magnificent day, in the world's creation history.

And as I've continued to read the predictions so dire
Of world annihilation, global warning, terrorists, the earth to expire
I see many glimmers of hope in the good deeds of women and men
Though far from perfection, in many ways doing well,
          since Original Sin.

And, while there is still prejudice, senseless killing, and atrocity,
There are threads of love, compassion, and reverence
          in man's philosophy.
And while we haven't reached the end of travesty and war,
There are many good things happening, our confidence to restore.

For we can take joy in the many advances that save men's lives
And we see generosity of people helping people, to the cynics'
      surprise.
And while the media blares nightly about man's inhumanity to man
I see others feeding the hungry, healing the sick, as best they can.

So, as I look to the future on this historic day,
I see bright rays of goodness, returning to God, along the way.
And, I shall continually look hopefully for the time to come
When there shall be peace in the valley, when darkness turns to sun.

The River of No Return

My eldest son, Jay, died October 28, 1980. The memory of that day, and the weeks, months, and years that have followed are burned in to my mind as if they happened yesterday. Yet his death also seems as if it happened in another life, another time. Anyone who has lost a child understands that, because life is never, can never be the same. We expect to lose our past (our parents), and even our present (our spouse), but we don't expect to lose our future (our children), in which we have placed our hopes and dreams. My son left us as two legacies, one of unimaginable pain and the other, wonderful memories, love, and many unexpected wonderful gifts, which I describe in "Blessings Come Forth." "The River of No Return" was written two years after Jay's death in commemoration of his passing. In it I seek to describe some of the phases we experienced in those two preceding years. This poem has been published previously in two national journals. We have given scores of copies to parents who have lost children, and will continue to do so. My hope is that it might give hope to any who are experiencing a grief or loss, and that it might give those who seek to help others in grief some understanding of what they are going through, and that even though they might have outrageous thoughts, they will be OK—in their own time—not someone else's schedule of recovery.

The River of No Return

I was cast into the cold and raging water
Suddenly, without warning, it's beyond belief
I thrashed about and denied it could happen.
Yet, it was I, in the River of No Return—grief.

No shortcuts, I must begin at the beginning
And pass through its treacherous course.
Battered by its many jagged rocks
Guilt, anger, doubt, a host of others, and remorse.

In those early days, I am numbed by the cold
By the shock of the loss of my precious loved one.
Scores of friends rush to the river's bank, casting out lifelines
But nothing can return my beloved, but lost, son.

These friends want so desperately to help,
But scarcely know what to say.
Then, some who have lost as we, enter the troubled waters
To reassure us, they understand, for they too, have passed this way.

The days become weeks, the gaping hole is still there
I cry out to God "Why? What have You done?
What have I done? When will the pain stop?
When will this journey end, this terrible river run?"

And then one day I see a ray of sun—
A day when things seem better, not all black.
Then, just as suddenly, I am dashed again on the sharp rocks
Of depression, despair, pain—it has all come back.

Again, one day I see a glimpse of truth
That many others have been here before me, are here now.
I am not alone in this river, and must finish its course
And yet, I am still filled with hurt and doubt.

41

The another insight one day comes to me
I can neither get out, nor turn back, I must pass through.
I cannot bury the hurts, the past, those dark corners
At last, I truly know what I must do—to pass through.

So, onward I go, knowing the river will have more raging rapids
But I shall work my way through, one day by one.
For as I do, I find there are those moments of peace, quiet eddies
When I feel again the joy—like warm rays of the sun.

Two years now, that I've traveled this River of Tears
While I know life won't be the same, I must let go the past.
To become stronger, more loving, caring and understanding
To reach out to touch those who've also been in this river cast.

I must tell them, each one, to have hope and heart
The River of Grief is hard, and when it seems you just can't take it
Reach up for inner strength, and accepting faith, reach out for help.
For as others have before you, you can make it.

And as I look back down the river's path I've gone
I was puzzled, and wondered why I did not drown.
Then, I realized, I was not alone, buoyed, carried, directed
By the God of Love, and through others help,
        was lost, but now am found.

Blessings Come Forth

Not long ago, I was asked to speak at the dedication of a memorial site for a regional Children's Cancer Center, established to remember children who had died. It is a place of peace and rest for the families of those whose children, brothers, sisters, and grandchildren have died.

I am sure I was selected, although that was not stated, because I well knew the pain of the loss of a child. It had been nearly twenty years since my son, Jay, had died, and as I began to reflect on his death once again, I knew that the loss is never over. Life is forever changed. There is not a day that goes by that my thoughts do not go back to my son's life and the joys and heartaches that we had. As I reflected once again on the last twenty years, I knew that many good things had come from my son's death, not because of it, but almost in spite of it. I realized that it is our attitude that makes the difference in any event. We must consciously decide to find good things and make good things from the trials of our life. We choose how we deal with and respond to crisis and troubles. If we choose to find and create good out of hurt—blessings will come forth.

Blessings Come Forth

It was twenty years ago, all my life was going so well
Then, in an instant, what was joy, turned to a living hell
For on that day, I received the news, that my son was dead.
The shock, the unbelief, how to tell my wife, spinning in my head.

"My son, my son!" from the depths of my soul I cry out.
All of those terrible feelings, the pain, guilt, and the doubt
Wrack my body and my soul, can anyone understand?
What I feel inside, I think my weeping shall never end.

Days, weeks, months pass, the cavernous hole still there
The loss, the questions of what if, and why, it's all so unfair.
Then one day, the thinking becomes so clear, in my insight
I can't change what happened, turn back the clock,
        to that one dark night.

I then realize that I must purpose, for myself and those I love,
        to make a choice
Whether 'tis better to be angry, feel pity, or let healing be my voice.
How grateful I am, I chose to seek the positive road for my life
For to have chosen anger and pity, would have bred
        cynicism and strife.

The recovery was sporadic, seemed interminable, ever so slow
But out of the ashes of my loss, yet a new life would grow.
Not that I wouldn't trade all I own, just to hear my son's voice
I must accept that such a trade, is neither an option nor a choice.

For out of my loss, I have found a depth of sensitivity, I never knew
To the pain and loss of others, the things they've gone through
And I've learned to treasure each day, that I may live
To focus on the present moment, to find what it is, that I may give.

I've come to know, how important are the people for whom I care
And express my love to them openly, things before I wouldn't dare.
I've learned that the greatest thing each of us can give or receive
Is our love and compassion, share others joy, and their pain relieve.

Yet another blessing came forth from my loss and my pain
Was to find and focus on the truly important things of life
      that sustain
The priorities of my life are now so different than before
All of the old goals of success, aren't so important anymore.

And I've learned that though death will steal our loved ones away.
Death cannot take way the precious memories, we treasure each day.
Even though twenty years have passed, these treasures
      are crystal clear
The love and life we shared, each day, each week, and each year.

So, I've found that even through the loss of my beloved son
He has left me many gifts, a legacy which I could not have won.
For how much richer is my life, even in his death.
How much I've learned, and may it continue 'til my last breath.

And yet with all the blessings from the ashes,
      that have come unto me
There are yet many questions, the answers, which I cannot see.
But a man once came to me, his Providential lesson to confide
"Don't fret," he said, "you'll have all the answers,
      when you meet Him, and him, on the other side."

Through Children's Eyes

There is an old saying "out of the mouths of babes," which tells us that often great truth and wisdom sometimes come innocently 'from the mouths of children. But what about children's eyes? This poem is to make us think about how much happier and more loving we would be as "big" people, if we would look at the world and life through children's eyes, rather than through the foggy vision we develop as adults. Adults' vision is often distorted by prejudice, formed opinions, fears, pride and judgments.

Through Children's Eyes

If only we could recapture the qualities of our youth.
If only we could retain the childlike joys, the simple truths.
If only we could once again see the world through children's eyes
The thrill of each day, the imagination and surprise.

A child is not so impressed with an expensive toy
But is happy with a cardboard box, an old spoon can bring him joy.
He's happy to watch an ant, with his heavy load and toil
To watch him build his home in the side yard soil.

He doesn't even notice his neighbors have more
Of the "things" that others have, he doesn't keep score.
For the number of toys to him, neither important nor sought
But learning and living life, the friends, the family,
        things that cannot be bought.

And in those around him he has complete trust
Because he hasn't yet learned, to be suspicious, you must.
For we teach him you must examine each other's agenda
Don't trust, or in the end you'll be hurt, this you must remember.

He has a curiosity about just how things work.
He'll study it for hours, to find each little quirk.
His imagination runs wild, building castles in the sand.
Thinking of ancient warriors in faraway lands.

And in his mind he pictures a blanket over a chair
Is a darkened cave, where he's safe from a lion, tiger, or bear.
He lies in the grass, studying the passing clouds in wonder
Sees an elephant, a dinosaur, a trampling horse amidst the thunder.

And when he speaks, he's honest, truthful, and without pretense
For he's not built around him the facades we have,
        that make no sense.
And even when he makes up a story, that he spins to you
His face shows it all, what he really feels, comes right through.

47

John Woolslair Sheppard

He wakes up each day, with a hilarious joy for living
His enthusiasm is contagious, positive vibrations he's giving.
He leaps from his bed, can't wait for the day to begin
Races through his day, never waiting to give up at its end.

He is so eager to learn, to observe and create
His little mind takes it all in, so quickly, never to abate.
But when he grows older, with all the mental barriers we've erected
He'll learn much more slowly, than his little open mind
       had projected.

To try anything win or lose, to take risks, he has no fear
He hasn't learned the world praises winners,
       second best is not so dear.
He'll learn from us, from great leaps of Faith, you must hold back
For if you try and fail, your performance they'll attack.

And from us he will meticulously learn to hate
All the things and people that we don't like, and berate.
For to him all people, all colors, all sizes are quite the same
All a part of humanity, our brothers, the strong, the feeble
       and the lame.

How I wish for a time when we might become children once more
When we could trust, be ourselves, not have to even the score,
A time when we could each drop the barriers and the masks
That separate us from each other, as we pursue life's tasks.

So may the time come when childish simplicity may reign
That we not look at others with suspicion and disdain
A time when each of us might see life through children's eyes
With joy, with love, with trust, in peace, each day a new surprise.

Scriptural references: Isaiah 11: 6–9; Matthew 18: 3–6

Prophets Without Honor

It has been said that an expert is a person who is at least twenty-five miles from home, wears a blue pinstripe suit, and carries an attache case. While the suit adds richness, and the attache case connotes knowledge and importance, the significant part of the triage, is the "away from home" factor. There is something to the saying that "familiarity breeds contempt." It refers to those that know us best—have seen our best and worst, but may more readily remember our shortcomings. And how could someone as imperfect as a hometowner know any more than we do?

Jesus experienced the phenomena when he returned Nazareth, which prompted Him to say, "Only in his hometown, among his own relatives, and in his own house . . . is a prophet without honor." (Mark 6:4)

The phenomenon is not new, and is clearly exemplified in the Gospel of Luke. When Jesus returned to his hometown of Nazareth, not only did his neighbors not accept him as a prophet, his own family thought He was insane. The hometowners gathered a lynch mob to throw him off a cliff. (Luke 4:23–30)

So if you have trouble at home with friends and family accepting your expertise in some area, take comfort, you are in excellent company.

Prophets Without Honor

A cobbler's children has no shoes to wear.
A barber's son lives with shaggy hair.
A lawyer who represents himself, has a client who's a fool.
That a doctor's child is always sickly, is the rule.

But one who was greater than all of these, in renown
Said a prophet is without honor in his own hometown.
What He meant in part, was familiarity breeds contempt
For those who know us best, our best efforts are often misspent.

There are many reasons why this might be so
Maybe because with those closest to us, only our love we bestow.
Or maybe it's because to be objective, with these, is most difficult
To give wise advice, and expect the desired result.

Or maybe, it's because, our human frailties, they've often seen
So that our advice, is viewed with our imperfect backdrop,
        with less esteem.
Or maybe, it's because it's easier to speak with another
        not so well known
Rather than with the one, with whom so much of our life
        has been thrown.

Or, maybe it's uncomfortable for them to fully confide
In one from whom their failures, they'd rather hide.
Whatever it be, it seems to be an almost universal law
It's tough to give advice, to those persons to whom we closest draw.

Even though we may find they don't hear, the best advice
        we've ever given.
They discover the same truth, comes from a stranger,
        seems to them God-given.
Just be happy, if they finally get the answer right.
Even though the memory of your same advice is out of sight.

This is not to say we shouldn't share with loved ones our best counsel
Because the wisdom we share, may well change their life
But whatever we say, must be with all gentleness and care—
Words carefully chosen, not to just correct, but to repair.

So don't feel discouraged, or like a failure you've been
When you can help total strangers to see the truth,
   yet not your own kin.
For if this be the case, join the club of the greatest One of all—
The Master, the Prophet, without honor, in His own town hall.

Listen

One of the most important gifts we are given is the gift of hearing. But there is a vast difference in hearing and listening. Listening involves understanding, comprehension, compassion, and taking in what another is saying, then responding to what has been said. Hearing then is a gift from God. Listening is a gift we can give to others, using the other gifts God has given us.

Listen

"Listen my children and you shall hear, of the midnight ride of
      Paul Revere."
Wise counsel, to hear *and* listen, from Longfellow, words which
      historians endear.
"Friends, Romans, countrymen, lend me your ears."
And from Shakespeare, words about listening intently, without peer.

When Paul and Art sang about "People hearing without listening"
And "People talking without speaking," there is something
      vital missing
Because listening is hearing with sensitivity, discernment and
      understanding
If we can learn to listen effectively, with others we'll enjoy
      great standing.

We need then to learn to listen more than we speak.
For in talking, we don't hear the inner cry of the down and weak
God gave us two ears and one mouth, for good reason
That we might listen, twice as much as we speak, in all seasons.

The ability to listen is one of the greatest gifts the Creator gives
To be able to do more than hear the words of a friend who lives
But to capture from the words, the deeper meaning of the
      spirit of another
Is a Love we can give, and bring us to them, closer than a brother.

So when someone speaks, listen with your ears, eyes, mind and
      your heart.
For the words may be but a mask of hurting feelings,
      of a life torn apart.
Seek then to read the face and listen to the body speak,
      to hear what they truly mean,
Then on your best judgment and wisdom, you must lean.

And having then listened with all of the tools, within you built in,
Choose your words thoughtfully, listening to that Small Voice within.
For having listened carefully, what you say, and do, in return
May change a life, your wise words teach, heal and confirm.

Waiting

Years ago, Samuel Beckett wrote a play titled "Waiting for Godot." The entire play is a dialogue between two characters who are waiting for a man named Godot. They wax long on how things will be different in their lives, when Godot comes. Many of us spend our lives "waiting for Godot" whether Godot is a person, a Mr. or Ms. Right, a new job, winning the lottery, a cure for disease, or whatever. Symbolically, "Godot" will make our lives better, if not complete. We wait for our children to come. We wait for them to grow up. We wait for them to leave home and become independent. We wait until we have enough to retire, or take that lifetime voyage. Many of us live in anticipation of the next stage or passage of our life. Sometimes in doing so, we don't even see what is going on around us and don't take time to enjoy the moment, while we are preoccupied with our waiting. "Waiting" suggests that like the two characters in "Waiting for Godot," we need to spend less time waiting and more time enjoying today, for who knows what tomorrow may bring?

Waiting

There is something about most of our lives that makes no sense
We spend much of our waking life, waiting for people,
    things and events.
And sometimes the people and things we wait upon, are no-shows
It's like waiting for our ship to come in, waiting for Godot.

When we're young each day is so long, as we wait for school to out
We watch the clock creep along, finally, we're out with a shout.
And as we get older, we just can't wait till we can drive
But when we finally do, parents wonder if we'll get home alive.

And, in these years we're waiting, looking for a mate just right
Then we find out it didn't work out, our relationship is a fright.
Then we've found the one to whom our life we'll submit
But even then, it's more waiting, till we have enough, it's a fit.

We make it through, we're expecting, the seeds have been sown
Our life to change, the months of waiting, for the new life we'll own.
We wait until she walks, she talks, she goes off to school.
Hurry up, get her dressed, take her, bring her home, run the carpool.

Now, we're waiting, worrying, until they leave, and even
    after I believe.
The time has come and gone, but the waiting's not over,
    there's no relief.
All the while we have strived in our business, to arrive at success
The grueling working hours, the finances, dealing with stress.

We've been working hard to put enough back, so we can retire
Oh, what fun it'll be, a home in the sun, golf, to this we aspire.
But when we get there, it's not quite as we thought, to finally relax
Only to find, we wish we'd all those wasted moments of
    waiting all back.

As we reflect, we see how pointless it is,
      waiting for our ship to come in
We see those lost moments, trying times , were wonderful in the end.
We never took time to enjoy, waiting for the next stage to come.
We've lived life, always anticipating, yet stressful and on the run.

So we need to not wait for what we are looking for tomorrow
But enjoy each moment we have, else we'll look back in sorrow.
For in our rushing and waiting, we're searching for elusive happiness
Only to realize, we had it each day, in our grasp, even
      amidst the stress.

What Price?

In my late twenties, I tried to understand what I believed about life and death, about God, and about my faith in a man named Jesus. I read the scriptures feverishly, I read books by theologians and writers, such as Karl Barth and C. S. Lewis (*Mere Christianity*). I went to Bible study classes led by a wonderful Christian teacher, who was the wife of a retired Army chaplain. I debated with myself the events of the Old and New Testament. But as I looked out as to how faith was lived out in the synagogues and the churches, I observed how complicated it seemed to become, with all of the laws and rules that different groups had. I saw how they argued with each other and judged each other when the other didn't accept their beliefs. And as I read more of the Gospels, it didn't seem all that complicated. It came down to some pretty basic stuff, such as honoring and worshipping God, loving and accepting ourselves, trying as best we could to love others, and to treat them fairly, honestly and with compassion. Then one day I came across a short passage in the Book of the Prophet Micah, which seemed to tie a lot of things together—at least about how we are to live out our lives. I won't hide it from you, it's Micah 6:6–8. "What Price?" is based upon that passage, and what God is asking of us in life. Even if you don't read "What Price?" go read Micah 6:6–8.

What Price?

What is it that God demands of us?
What is it we are to give, without a fuss?
The answer is important, there's so much at stake
Does He want a third, or half, or all that I make?

With what will He be content, what is sufficient?
With all that I've received, anything given, totally deficient?
Would silver, gold, a thousand head of cattle be just enough?
Or ten thousand barrels of oil, a thousand diamonds in the rough?

The truth is He never asked us for a given sum,
He asks for our tithe, helping others, things to be done.
He asks that we do justice, love mercy, be humble before Him
All with an attitude of gentleness, humility each day, to our end.

For all that we are, that we have, comes from Him.
All our treasure, our talents, our family and our friends
Have been entrusted to us as tenants, sojourners while we are here.
All these gifts, and life, are from God, these things we hold dear.

It seems so simple to revere God, do mercy, and be just
But applying it each day, tis not easy, but try we must.
Each day I shall strive, in all, to do the right things
That I may commit my life, my gifts, all to His honor to bring.

Scripture references: Micah 6: 6–8; 1 Chronicles 29 12–16

Unto the Least of Them

In the Gospel of Matthew, Chapter 25, the Master is talking to His disciples, giving them instruction for the future. He tells them that when the Son of Man comes in His glory He will separate the "sheep from the goats" and will tell those on His right that they have come into their inheritance because when He was in prison, they visited Him, when He was thirsty, they gave Him drink, when He was hungry, they fed him. They asked, "When were you ever hungry, thirsty, and in prison—and we did those things for you?" He answered them by saying whenever you do things for others in need, it is just as if you've done it to Me, your teacher, your leader and your friend. But sometimes our thirst, our hunger and our imprisonment may be more than physical, but emotional, mental or spiritual. We are able to and need to help others in their need, as we are able. Often we find that the giver is as enriched than the recipient, because of the benefits we receive in giving. "Unto the Least of Them" is about giving with a purpose—about helping others.

Unto the Least of Them

As I pondered life's meaning, through one dark night
As I viewed a wicked world, with wrong consuming right
It was then I thought upon that wondrous sight
O Jesus's outstretched hands, His love, without respite.

I was sick, weary, homeless, and You took me in.
You bound up my wounds, and washed away my sin.
I was down and out, a stranger, You became my friend.
Naked and you clothed me, from without and within.

I lay in darkened prisons, and You visited me.
Entombed in the fears of my inner self, for infinity
You showed me the Father of lights, that I might see
That life can have meaning, even in me.

My body, frail and empty, you gave me food to eat.
Cool water for my thirst, then stood me on my feet.
That Living Water, that covenant of love, so sweet
You gave me the kingdom's victory, took away my defeat.

With strong and beckoning arms, He calls, "Come unto me
All of you who are heavy laden, My peace, I give to thee
For My yoke is light my burden light, I'll take your burdens,
        that you might be
My child, my friend, my brother, and I will love you for eternity."

The hosts of heaven will shout a great "Amen!"
When we have learned the lessons taught, when God, His Son,
        walked among men
For when we've cast our burdens on Him, done these things
        unto the least of them
Through Jesus love and life, we've done it unto Him.

Scriptural reference: Matthew 25: 35–45; Matthew 11: 28–30

A Prayer of Thanksgiving

Our family gathers together each year for a grand meal and celebration at Thanksgiving. While we always give a blessing and prayer of thanks while holding hands, several years ago I felt a special need that we had not truly reflected on things we should be thankful for. It was then for this special day that this prayer was written.

A Prayer of Thanksgiving

I lift my prayer and praise, to my Father, my God
Who has been with me through the mountains and valleys I've trod.
He who is my only Redeemer, the beginning and the end
Who sent forth His Son, to save my soul, and be my friend.

I give to Thee my thanks, Thy praises I sing
For the gift of life, for loved ones and family, the joys they bring
Each day that I have, is but a gift to me.
May I live each day, as best I can, to honor Thee.

I pray that my life might have meaning and purpose
That my faith lived out, shall be much more than just surface
That people might see your righteous Son in me
That He gave His very life, all to set me free.

I pray that I shall never forget, all that I am, that I have, aren't mine
But that I am just the steward, the tenant, of what is truly Thine.
For my talents, my treasure, my body and my mind
Are to be used to help others, for Your glory, and as your sign.

Bless those around me that they may come to know
It is through our faith in Thee, that we truly grow.
That they may know that each life in Your eyes has great worth
That we are placed here for a purpose, from the date of our birth.

So I thank you Lord for the life and gifts I've received
Which, as I reflect, have greater worth than I ever perceived
And, I'm thankful for those who've accepted and loved me.
For love is from you, You are love, from the beginning to eternity.

Amen.

The Demands on Man

"The Demands on Man" covers the same subject as "The Price" and comes from the question asked in Micah 6: 8, but takes a slightly different tack.

The Demands on Man

What is it that my Creator wants of me?
I've often pondered and thought on this mystery
Will He be satisfied, if I become king
Or president, or a captain of industry?

Will He be pleased, if I conquer the world
In all the nations, with my banners unfurled?
If I gain great status, position or power
Have the accolades of men on me showered?

Or would it be for me His desire
That men call me rich, to that I should aspire?
For surely if I have the praise of men
He would be honored, and pleased with me then.

Or, how much of my treasure will it take?
Does He want it all, make or break
Would He be content, with say ten percent, or half?
Or will a sacrifice be sufficient, a fatted calf.

And as I have searched, I have come to see
It is not my treasure that He demands of me.
For I cannot buy His pleasure at any price
Not even with great inventions, or sage advice.

For He has told us what He asks of us.
It seems so simple, not a lot of fuss.
He asks that we do justice, with all whom we live
To be loving, compassionate, understanding, and forgive.

Finally, He asks that my life's walk, be humbly with Him
To acknowledge my need of Him, through thick and thin.
To blend my talents and treasure with love, without cease.
His promise, if I give my first fruits, my silos will increase.

65

John Woolslair Sheppard

I've found that all the treasures, power, and expensive toys
Are not the things that bring us inner peace and joy.
For those things are but passing, and do not last
Love is the answer to our future, our present and our past.

Money

"Money" needs little explanation. It is easy to have the illusion that "once our ship comes in" we will have happiness, security, and all of the "good" things in life. Not only does money not bring these things, but often money brings the opposite result. For in our quest for happiness, security, and the good things in life that can be purchased with money, those very things often slip away from us. "Money" is a series of short two-line anamorphic statements about what money can and can't do.

Money

Money can buy a bed
But not sleep.

Money can buy books
But not knowledge, intelligence or wisdom.

Money can buy food
But not feed the hungry mouths.

Money can buy beautiful clothes
But not inner beauty.

Money can buy a house
But not make a home.

Money can buy medicine
But not total health.

Money can buy luxuries
But not integrity.

Money can buy amusement
but not happiness.

Money can buy a laborer
But not a friend.

Money can buy a relaxing vacation
But not inner peace.

Money can buy your love expensive rings
But not her love.

Money can buy your children expensive toys
But not their respect.

Money can buy a church pew
But not a ticket to heaven.

Money can buy a religious sacrifice
but cannot buy atonement.

Money can buy a Bible or religious symbol
But cannot buy a savior.

Does this mean, that money is all bad?
If so, then for all our efforts, 'tis very sad.

Money, as all things entrusted to us—simply a tool.
Use it wisely and for good, or become a fool.

To Be or Not To Be

Sometime ago, I prepared a video text for a charitable organization on giving consideration to the legacy that a person leaves. The video was about choices we have in life. "To Be or Not To Be" follows much of the text, that is, it is not just about choices, but more about attitude, about ourselves, about others, about our life.

The writing begins with Hamlet's rhetorical question in which he was talking about his own existence. In "To Be" we take the verb "to be" and develop it into attitudes about our approach to life.

To Be or Not To Be

"To be or not to be," that is not, as Hamlet said, a question.
It is your choice, to be as you will be, it is your direction.
You may choose to think and live life with a helping positive attitude
And if you do, you will bring in your life satisfaction and gratitude.

Or, you can choose to be angry, confrontational, and negative
To blame others for the cards you're dealt, as the way you live.
But 'tis better to be comfortable with where and who you are
For then your life will have meaning, and you will go far.

With this in mind, may I the suggest a route for you
To pattern your life's journey, in all that you do.
Even though these thoughts won't all of life's problems resolve
But may they help you each day, with the tasks you're involved.

Think positively in all that you do
Think on the good things, not dwell on the bad
Think of how you can, instead of why you cannot.
Think, truth, think forgiveness, think love.

Be Thankful, for who you are and the talents you have been given.
Be Considerate, try to understand where the other is coming from.
Be Encouraging, even when there may be little to encourage.
Be Instructive, when you have knowledge or wisdom to impart.
Be Humble in your attributes, your accomplishments,
        and possessions.
Be Giving, for what you have has been entrusted to you.
Be Perceptive, there is a whole world going on around you.
Be Aware, that life is precious, time is passing, use it wisely
        and for good.
Be Understanding to all, to the best of your ability.

Don't Hesitate to say I don't know, I made a mistake, or I'm sorry.
Don't Criticize others, until you've walked in their shoes.
Don't Make Judgments, until you know you have all the facts.
Don't Say anything, unless you can say something constructive.
Don't Build yourself up, by tearing others down.
Don't Worry about tomorrow—today has enough problems of its own.

Realizing, that in all of these things, you will often fall short.
Always strive for and ask for excellence—not perfection.
Always leave things better than you found them.
Finally, when your life is done, leave a heritage that others
        can build on.

Learning to Laugh

Solomon, reputed to be the wisest man in history, tells us, "A happy heart is like good medicine, but a broken spirit drains your strength." (Proverbs 17:22) And, "As a face is reflected in water, so the heart reflects the person." (Proverbs 27:19) Laughter, then, is good for the body and good for the soul. "Learning to Laugh" is about making laughter a part of our life, not only to make our life happier, but also to help us mentally, physically, and spiritually. What each of us needs is six good belly laughs a day, to keep the doctor away.

Learning to Laugh

A heart that is joyful is reflected in a cheerful face
A pleasant smile and laugh, exudes an internal grace.
And when your thoughts and mind are angry and mad
These negative vibrations overcome our heart, and make it sad.

A good case of laughter, is contagious, and medicine for the soul
It will keep our life from becoming too drab and too droll.
Pleasant words are as a honeycomb to the bee
While our affirming words give joy, for the world to see.

So we need to find those things that bring us to laugh
For in laughter and joy, we cut the negative, at least in half.
Find then your funny bone, and tickle it each day
And you'll find life's journey a more pleasant path, along the way.

If we take our life and our circumstances, all too grave
It will affect our demeanor, and the way we behave.
We need to laugh at ourselves daily, who and where we are
Lest we come to feel too much our importance, reaching for our star.

And careful of our laughter at others, lest we inflict on them pain
What we say and do, will build up or tear down,
        may show our disdain.
There is a difference in pointing out the humor of another's ways
And laughing together, a jab at all of our follies, all of our days.

Learning to laugh, then can bring joy to our hearts,
        and help mend our hurt.
It can wash away the negative thoughts, and hurtful actions divert.
Laughter is relaxing, makes us healthy, and dissolves our tensions
Will give us a new look at life, and a pleasant new dimension.

The Greatest Gift

"The Greatest Gift" is another poem, along with "The Advocate," that was written for my friend James D. Newton. I completed "The Advocate" in early December 1999. Jim, who was terminally ill, and his wife, Ellie, were so appreciative of my effort that I determined to write a Christmas gift for them. The greatest gift anyone has to give to another is the gift of love. I finished the poem, and planned to take it to Jim and Ellie the next week, which was a few days before Christmas. However, Jim died during the weekend. I delivered my poem to Ellie on my first visit to her following Jim's death, along with a small box of her favorite candy–Godiva Chocolates. She told us later that while she loved the chocolates, the greatest gift she had received were found in the words of the poem.

The Greatest Gift

As we reflect upon the life that we are living
And examine the goals we seek in achieving,
There is only one mark that will truly stand out
The aim that taps the depths of what we are about.

The greatest ends aren't as the world might believe
The financial, political, or personal successes we achieve.
For while these are the marks the world uses to measure.
Surely, these shall not be the ones that we most treasure.

All of the silver and gold, the control and the power
Will in their own time, rust, fade and sour.
For those treasures which are truly most sought
Can neither be traded, bartered nor bought.

It is Love given and received from spouse, child and friend
It is knowledge of a life of integrity, that prevails to the end
It is a life of acceptance of Self, that brings inner Peace
And not, the never ceasing and seeking of vanity, that brings release.

For Love is the Truth that shall set us free
Love is the force that connects us to eternity.
Love—the most precious gift we receive and give
It is Love that gives us joy, and the will to live.

It is in our love, that we reach to Heaven above
For Love is of God, and God, through us, is Love.
And, yet knowing this, it is to me an eternal mystery—
This simple Truth, that God knowing me fully, could Love even me.

Through God's Love, He takes us to his kingdom,
     not as a stranger.
Yet, His greatest gift of Love to the world, a wee child in a manger
And, His greatest gift to me, that my life and my death,
     be not for loss,
Letting His Son die, His blood His pain, for my failures,
     nailed to a Cross

May I, then, come to know, the greatest gift I have to give
From the beginning of my life and each day that I live.
Is Love, which is God, and through which He is in me,
That others may come to know Him, through me, for eternity.

Scriptural references: Matthew 16: 26; Matthew 25: 35;
1 Corinthians 13; John 8: 32, 1 John 4:7–21,
Ecclesiastes 1:2 "Vanity of vanities! All is vanity."

Sometimes

"Sometimes" is about the "sometimes" of life—sometimes things are one way, sometimes another. This is yet another writing about the idea that there is a time for most things—the key is knowing what time it is. This poem uses the anaphora method, using the repetitive word "sometimes."

Sometimes

Sometimes I'm in a great rush to achieve or get somewhere.
And often, I find, I don't know where I am when I get there.
Sometimes, life is such a rush, I just want to stop and get out.
It's then, in this frantic world, I wonder what it's all about.

Sometimes, I'm really focused, have many goals to achieve.
I'm so organized, have it all together, or so I believe.
But then sometimes, nothing seems to fall in place.
At those times it seems whatever I do, I'll fall on my face.

Sometimes the days go so well, oh how I enjoy
All the lessons of life, I so readily employ.
But then, sometimes, it seems that nothing goes right
Absolutely nothing comes together, try as I might.

And sometimes, I've found it important the right words to speak,
But at other times, I know tis best, my silence to keep.
Sometimes are the times when people, ideas, and love
     I must embrace,
But there are sometimes, when I must let go, their release
     I must face.

Sometimes the big things that had seemed so important to me,
I found in time were inconsequential, would wash out to sea
Then, sometimes, I realize the loves I'd come to take for granted
Were and are to me, most important, my greatest
     commitment demanded.

In all of life, then, I've learned, there is a sometime for everything
The highs and lows of life, bells of gladness and sorrow to ring.
So it is, then I must learn from each of my sometimes,
     in joy and in strife
To appreciate in love all of these sometimes, that are a part of our
     life.

Tomorrow

There was a popular song in the 1950s titled "Mañana." The lyrics proclaimed that "tomorrow is soon enough for me." Why do today, what you can put off until tomorrow? "Tomorrow" specifically focuses on putting off saying something that should be said to someone. But, the principle of procrastination applies to all areas of our lives—those things we want to do or ought to do, but put off because they may be unpleasant or uncomfortable. So, "Tomorrow" is about procrastination. It's easy to say we will do something tomorrow, but often tomorrow never comes. Do it today, then it's not a part of tomorrow's worries—because it's done.

Tomorrow

Tomorrow is in the future, and so is next week.
There are so many things to do, so many things to seek.
So many things tugging at me, that I need to do
I just haven't found the time, to speak to you.

There are letters to write, errands to run, calls to make,
But there are things I wanted to say to you, for heavens sake.
I really do care, but I scarcely know where goes the time
My motives are good, but it just seems my time is not mine.

I've thought it all through, considered it, in and out
I know what I need to do or say, without a doubt.
Yet each day I put it off, it's more difficult to do.
Surely tomorrow will be the right time for me and for you.

Or maybe it's just that I just don't really know what to say
The things I've wanted to tell you for so long, without delay.
I've so treasured our friendship, may the right words come, I pray.
Oh, if I could only do it, right now, today.

Another day is gone, many reasons I didn't get it done.
Maybe I'll do it tomorrow, before another day has run.
And yet I worry, that in what I say, I may be the fool
I should just tell you what I feel, let my conscience rule.

I must resolve to say and do what's on my heart today
Whether it's my love, my concern, a doubt, or a dispute
        along the way.
For all I have is the moment, today, there's no assurance of
        tomorrow.
To leave things unsaid, undone, when comes our last,
        would leave sorrow.

It's Time—To Fast

"It's Time—To Fast" is a play on words using the words "to" and "too" along with the word "fast," which also has several meanings. Interestingly, the word "fast" has at the same time opposite meanings—one meaning speed, and the other meaning to slow down or hold back (such as restricting or refraining from eating). So, the poem asks the question "What time is it?" Is it time "to fast" or is it a time "too fast?" My observation is that the time we are living in is both a time "too fast" and a time "to fast."

It's Time—To Fast

It's that time, but is it time to fast, or time too fast.
For to fast means to hold back, to hang on to the past.
While too fast means we are speeding, as through life
To fast will slow us down, but too fast brings stress and strife.

I submit, this is a time of living too fast, not living to fast.
Everything, everybody, lives in a rush, the die is cast.
Just look around you, and there's never any time
To stop and rest, smell the roses, enjoy the sublime.

We live on a fast treadmill, keep running, never stop.
We've got fast pace, fast food, fast cars, look out for the cop.
We've got fast service, fast flights, fast credit, fast pain relief.
We want fast track approval, fast profits, where's the beef?

We've got fast cell phones, fast computers, fast money at the ATM.
We just don't have time to stop, a minute to wait, that'd be a sin.
Where in the world are we going, that we have to get there so fast.
If we don't get instant gratification or relief, we feel harassed.

Maybe it's time to change and switch from too fast to—to fast
Slow down, savor the moment and enjoy life, make it last
Or, one day we may find we've raced through life from
        beginning to end.
Look back, not knowing where we've been, we've missed life
        and its dividends.

Just Like My Dad

All of us who have children are concerned about what they learn and what they will become. What we often fail to realize is that they learn more from watching us—and other big people. They learn the most, not by what we say, but by what we do, and who we are. And the learning, unfortunately for us, isn't over when we send them out of the nest (or they leave or just fall out—or never leave). They keep on watching, as the poem suggests, until our last breath. That is truly an awesome responsibility that is placed on parents, and grandparents. It doesn't stop there. You or I may be the de facto parent for someone else, a role model without knowing it. You may just be the best person someone else knows. How are you living it out?

Just Like My Dad

A young boy I know was passing by, stopped to visit me one day
A talkative vibrant lad, I'd always listen to what he had to say.
That day we talked about many things, life, girlfriends and sports
Talked about his friends at school, having fun with his cohorts.

After we'd talked awhile, I posed a question, just for him
Asked what he'd like to be, who he'd be like, when he became a man.
He thought a moment, then said he'd like to be just like his dad.
Loved his dad, he was gone a lot, things sometimes hard,
        made him sad.

And here is what he said:

"I want to drive cars aggressive and fast, beat red lights,
        and look out for cops,
Just like my dad.

I want to cut sharp deals, even if I have to shave the truth,
        to hit the top,
Just like my dad.

I want to have a bunch of credit cards, so I can get everything
        I want,
Just like my dad.

I want to learn to party, maybe get drunk at night,
        frequent the evening haunts
Just like my dad

I want to smoke, maybe chew too, and try other stuff,
        because it's cool,
Just like my dad.

I want a wife to wait on me, I'll do what I must to keep her in line,
        follow my rule,
Just like my dad.

I'll give my kids money and things, but I'll be real busy,
        won't have much time,
Just like my dad.

I'll fudge a little on taxes and business, it's OK, just to
        make things right, so I get mine,
Just like my dad.

If things get tough at home, I'll get somebody else,
        or maybe just leave for awhile,
Just like my dad.

It's going to be fun when I grow up, I'll get just what I want for me,
        nothin' to cramp my style,
Just like my dad.

Though the story is stretched, yet my young friend is like most boys,
        looking up to his dad,
Especially in their younger years, they'll watch every movement,
        habit and fad.
The way we act, the things we say and do, are indelibly stamped
        on their little brains.
They see right through us, see what we do, and say, see us as we are,
        not how we may feign.

Whether our children are young or older, like it or not,
        we're models for them,
How we treat others, how we do business, whether dishonesty
        we condemn.
Younger eyes are watching our every move, how we deal with
        things of life and death.
It's an awesome responsibility, our life lived out, will be our legacy,
        to our last breath.

Who is This Man?

Jesus of Nazareth lived two thousand years ago. Two millennium later people are still asking the question of who and what He was, and who and what is He today. If we read the scripture closely, we aren't given much wiggle room about Him. As C. S. Lewis, in *Mere Christianity* suggests, either "He was who he said He was, or He was a lunatic, akin to someone who claims to be a fried egg." In other words, we can't take a middle ground that he was a great teacher, philosopher, or thinker, but not who He claimed to be. The choice then is up to us. Or, we can elect not to even consider the choice. That is the option Someone gave us when we were given a mind, and the ability to choose our beliefs. What do you think?

Who is This Man?

Who is this man, from far across the sea
This man, who lived and died, in tiny Judea and Galilee?
T'was two thousand years ago, He proclaimed a new belief.
The impact of His life, so simple yet profound, to bring joy, relief.

There is no person who influenced the world's thinking more
Than this Man of Sorrows, from Nazareth, on Galilee's shore.
Though He hung from a cross, with criminals, centuries ago
His life and words are alive today, still set lives aglow.

He spoke of love, giving and sharing, to all who would hear.
Said the Great Creator loved all of his children, to Him so dear.
He spoke of forgiveness, that He would give up His life
Promised a new life, a new world coming, without strife.

Yet some said He was a fraud, a magician, the leader of a cult
Others said He was a rebel, a man without a father, words of insult
Some said He was blasphemous, in the claims that He made
Others said He was a satanic antichrist, should make men afraid.

He asked his followers, what others were about Him saying.
They answered, "Some say John the Baptist, Jeremiah,
        or Elijah praying."
He asked all of them, then, "Who do you say that I am?"
"Thou art the Christ, the Son of Living God," answered only one man.

But He died ignominiously on a cross, on one dark day
For the failures of many, then as now, our price He would pay.
Those who knew Him, claimed in three days He rose from the dead.
He said that He had died for others, now and forever, gave
        His life instead.

But, who do people say that He is, in this troubled world today
Some say a prophet, a great teacher, who had charisma,
    with people to sway.
But with the things He said, the claims He made,
    He is either Savior or master of deceit.
We must either call Him insane, or call Him, Master,
    and fall at His feet.

And, when He asks me the question, "Who do you say that I AM?"
I'll call Him Lord, my Comforter, my Strength and my Redeemer,
    the Sacrificial Lamb.
I'll call Him Grace, Love, King of Kings, my hope and my shield.
I'll call Him my shelter, my friend and the shepherd of my life,
    to Him shall I yield.

I ask you then if you know Him, He who healed minds and souls,
    this man from Galilee.
This man who lived long ago, He who lives today, for those
    who seek him, even me.
And, if you don't know Him, He stands at your door, to meet you,
    on this very day.
He gives new eternal Life freely, will love you unconditionally,
    never to stray.

Scripture reference Matthew 16: 13–16.

John Woolslair Sheppard

The Eye of the Beholder

My wife, Ellen, is an artist. Like so many artists, she is very seldom satisfied with her work. She works and reworks her art, and often destroys a work in frustration when she feels she has "mudded" it. Then sometimes almost with a wisp of the brush, she creates a beautiful painting.

I am not an artist. I can't even draw a stick figure so that anyone will know what it is. But I know what I perceive is beauty. And much of what I see in art is neither artistic nor beautiful. But what do I know? I only know what pleases me.

And, while I make constructive criticisms to my wife on her work, by and large, I see everything she paints as having grace and beauty. I have come to realize that I would like most anything she does because I love her. But I believe my eyes are not blinded by my love, but rather that because of that love I find beauty in what my eyes see. There is beauty in everything, animal, vegetable, God created or man created, since man is created in the image of God. It is simply that too often, we are blinded by our life experience, our preconceived idea of beauty, or our prejudices to see the beauty in everything. And it is love that opens our eyes to see what we might otherwise miss entirely. Through love, what we would only see through a window dimly, we see more clearly, and behold beauty face to face.

Years ago I read a magazine article about a man who entered his work in a regional art exhibit. In his putter room, he had an old piece of canvas on the floor. Through the years he had walked on it, did building projects and sanded on it, wiped paint brushes and spilled paint on it. He mounted his canvas floor mat, framed it and placed it in the exhibit. His work was critically acclaimed by the judges and art critics. Only later did he reveal his artistic secret. Beauty, indeed, is in the eye of the beholder!

The Eye of the Beholder

They say that wisdom comes with age
If that be so, then I should be an enlightened sage.
One thing I've learned, though as I've grown older,
Is that beauty, truly, is in the eye of the beholder.

We look for beauty in the wonders of nature
Or in the supple female body, with just the right curvature.
Sometimes we find beauty in the lope of a graceful animal
At other times in something packaged large, sometimes small.

Others find beauty in the magnificent art of the great masters
While some one else, discovers it, in what seems
          thrown-together plaster.
One will tell you fine art is only to be found in the strokes
          of impressionism.
But if he speaks to a Dali enthusiast, there'll be between them
          a great schism.

The truth is that we can find beauty in any person, animal,
          plant, or thing
For the stonecutter, beauty is found in a rock, for another
          a sunset makes the heart sing.
One may see beauty in a red-faced newborn child,
          another in a crippled old man.
And, admiring affection will transform a child's messy painting
          to a Gauguin.

How is it then, that in beauty and grace, we have such
          contrasting views.
Observe the same artistic work, one sees junk, another marvels at
          the strokes and hues.
There is then artistry in all things, on surface or within.
          Each is God's or man's creation
Its appeal or not, is governed by whether heart and mind
          join with eyes in adoration.

It is love though, that truly opens the eye to find the beauty
    in anything.
For love looks out and in, finds the good and the beautiful,
    makes a pauper into a king.
So beauty is subjective, depends upon what is in the perceiver's
    heart and mind
Enables the eye to see through all imperfections, 'tis fallacy
    when it's said "love is blind."

A Game of Cards

Recently I was talking to one of my grandsons, who had just undergone major surgery on his shoulder as a result of a sports injury. He is a baseball player, and the shoulder was that of his throwing arm. The surgeon made no assurances of his future in sports. We talked about his shoulder and life, and how we don't always know what tomorrow holds, how things change, and how the "cards" we receive are not always fair. We have to take the cards we are dealt and play them out as best we can with what we have. Some cards we can choose, others we receive, want them or not. Some are a treasured gift, others a challenge. We all receive wanted and unwanted cards, and our job is to play each to the best of our ability. That is all anyone can ask. I know that he has, and will, continue working and playing the cards he has, to the best of his ability. "A Game of Cards" is about this idea.

John Woolslair Sheppard

A Game of Cards

Life in many ways is like a continuing card game
Each person dealt a different hand, none quite the same.
In a sense then, life is like a game of five card draw
Except we're dealt many cards of life, some large, some small.

And some cards we can turn down, exchange, others we must hold.
Some of our cards may make us weep, while others make us bold.
The structures of our bodies are keepers, our genes, size,
        color, and look
Things we're born with, our gifts, didn't ask for, can't change,
        by hook or crook.

I'd love to have the talent height and strength of a Jordan or a Shaq
But to try to jump like those two, I'd end up on my back.
Some unwanted cards drawn later, crippling accidents, like
        Christopher Reeve's
Are cards of overcoming, could their courage or patience, I achieve.

Some cards are cards of opportunity, some cards supremely
        test our will
Some cards we draw daily, some like mountains to climb,
        others, a mole hill
Some cards we choose to draw, as to others we have no choice.
Some cards painful, make us sad, with others we'll rejoice.

On those cards of life, we have options on which to choose
We need to select thoughtfully, and not our choices misuse
And if we find they don't play out, be willing to change again.
The right timing to exchange those cards is an art,
        the how and the when.

The game goes on night and day, our lifetime throughout.
There will be times of plenty and harvest, and times of drought.
Our job is to play out the cards we're dealt,
      along with those we select.
The very best that we can, to bring about a positive effect.

A choice we do have is, as to which suite in which we play.
Whether it be spades, clubs, diamonds, or hearts, our lives to inlay.
Choose hearts, play all your cards, with love, integrity,
      help and compassion.
At games end, you'll have won with a royal flush,
      from your cards of life fashioned.

Worry, Let it Be

Worry is a national epidemic. Billions of dollars are spent each year on medical help and over-the-counter headache remedies. Although there are different kinds of headaches, such as migraine and cluster headaches, the common stress headache is most prevalent. And, in most cases stress is brought on by worry. Worry about what we did or said, or didn't do or say yesterday, or what is going to happen tomorrow.

The word worry is derived from a German word würgen, which means to choke or strangle. That is exactly what worry does to us—to choke or strangle the joy out of life, if not life itself. Worry creates stress, and stress has been proven to be a major factor in stroke and heart attack. You can't change the past, but you can ruin your present by worrying about the future. Having said all of that, do I worry? Absolutely. Do you worry? For sure. In fact, some families have "designated" worriers, who just worry all the time. So in those families, the others can be Alfred E. Newmans and say "What me, worry?"

We need to take worry out and look at it for what it is, and see what it does to us, and understand that worry never accomplished one iota of good, or solved a single problem. All it really does is make us miserable and less effective human beings. Realizing then, that we probably won't completely eliminate worry, but at the very least, we need to take control of our worries, and by doing that, take control of and make our daily lives better.

Worry, Let it Be

"In my times of trouble, Mother Mary speaks to me
Singing words of wisdom, let it be, let it be."
So sang the Beatles, nearly forty years now past
But the ancient message of letting go our anxiety, will surely last.

For worry does nothing to solve the things that trouble
Often merely breaks us down, turns our life into rubble
To worry comes from würgen which means to strangle, or to choke
But to one who lives with worry daily, it is clearly not a joke.

Worry begins, almost as a droplet of water, a thought
Develops into a continuing stream, from that one thought wrought.
And if we let it, it becomes an obsessive raging flood
Will dominate of our lives, unless we seize control of it,
      nip it in the bud.

Worry about what is past is folly, for it's done
We can't relive or change yesterday, there is no time rerun.
We can correct what we can, learn from mistakes,
      do it different next time.
But we can't take back the lost moment, retrieve words spoken,
      never in a lifetime.

And, worry about tomorrow or the future, is also futile.
Worry never solved a problem, and things may change, meanwhile
Many times, we find in our worry about the future, the anticipation
Is, more often than not, much worse than our worry's realization.

So, just deal with the problems that stand before you today
Tomorrow's problem, will find tomorrow's solution, along the way
If, then, we confront today's problems today, at any rate,
And do it right, we'll already have taken on a full plate.

It may help our angst, to know that while we can completely control
    a few things
There are other matters, in which we may have some say,
    but not resolution bring.
There are yet many more situations, over which we have zero
    dominion or deliverance.
May these truths ease our anxieties, and may we have the wisdom
    to know the difference.

Worry never passed a test, paid a bill, or cured a disease.
It never worked a job, slew Goliath, or defeated Hercules.
In all of history, worry never accomplished a single thing
But to make us less effective, and to our doubts cling.

So, when worry comes to knock at your mind's door
Simply say, no thanks, I have no need of you anymore.
Knowing that worry has nothing to offer or benefit you
That things will go better, without adding worry, to life's milieu.

In Praise of All Working Mothers

I have always been in awe of the mountainous undertaking of being a mother. Mothers suffer the pain, discomfort, and burden of carrying the child through nine months of pregnancy, and from the child's first breath, seem to have never-ending work. Have you seen winning athletes who get their fifteen minutes of glory on television say "Hi, Mom!" to their mothers? And how many times do we hear testimonials of people who have "arrived" credit their mother? That's not to say that dads aren't important. In fact, I believe one of the underlying causes of many of the family and societal problems we face today are because of the lack of a strong fatherly image in so many homes. But moms—they're the best!

I also have a beef against those who would put down the "stay at home" mom—the one who fights in the trenches of raising children twenty four hours a day. Granted, many mothers aren't given an economic choice—they must work out of the home. I have special praise for those mothers who have a choice, and choose to stay at home and put their full focus on their home and their children. God bless them! They need all of the support and affirmation they can get, for it's often a thankless task—not appreciated by their spouse, their children, nor society in general.

My grandmothers, my mother, my wife, my daughter, and my daughter-in-law have all been stay-at-home moms. Much is expected of them their entire life. Their job is never done. I retired several years ago. My wife has never, nor will she ever retire. The work goes on. When my children were young, I resented the fact that when there was a "mother" job to be done, that some of the children's friends would always say, "Ask Mrs. Sheppard, she doesn't work." She did work, and still works, as hard and as diligently as any mother, "working" or not. Her life has been just more focused. So this is in praise of all mothers, who work, but especially for those who are full-time mothers.

In Praise of All Working Mothers

It won't take you long to figure where I'm coming from
For I lift this in praise of all working moms.
First, for those who work for career, by divorce or by choice
For all of these working moms, I lift my appreciative voice.

For those whose husbands or lovers left without a trace.
For those who have to face the world alone, face to face.
For those who have husbands, but must work for family support.
For those who raise the children, whether they're happy,
      or out of sorts.

To those who must place their children in child care, five days a
      week.
To those who get up at dawn, return at dusk, in pursuit of
      a living wage to seek.
To those who manage home and work, and are exhausted at bedtime.
To those who grasp on weekends, the moment with their children,
      quality time.

These moms are folks who must function at many tasks,
      for better or for worse,
Sometimes wife, sometimes employee, sometimes parent,
      sometime nurse,
Balancing her time between the commands of job and demands
      of home
Pulled in all directions, with precious little time in which to
      call her own.

So, don't misunderstand me, the "work-out-of-the-home mom,"
      is really great
There is something I would like to add about moms,
      to be perfectly straight
The "stay-at-home-mom," works just as hard, focusing all her
      energies on the ones
That she brought into the world, involved in every detail of home,
      'til day is done.

Twenty-four hours, for eighteen years and more,
  she does the burping, diapering feats.
The boo-boo kissing, scolding, praising, fight mediation,
  school deadlines to meet.
School visits, little league, trips, science projects, finding lost jackets
Allergies, sore throats, infected ears, Halloween costumes,
  and music racket.

Santa Claus lists and gifts, remote control cars, first bras,
  curfews, driving lessons,
Sweetheart screening, fixing the meals, speeding tickets,
  teenage obsessions,
The right clothes, monitoring TV and movies, talking things out,
  and nightmares,
Bathroom and telephone hoarding, driving lessons,
  and teenage speechless stares.

The above, just a few of the day/night job of the mom who stays
  at home.
Her job is not as exciting as the career mom, and often is a drone.
But maybe even more important, because she's totally in charge
  of our most precious gift
Full time, so lets hear it for the "stay-at-home-mom,"
  and give her a lift.

When Life Seems Unfair

I recently read an Associated Press article that appeared in newspapers across the country about a young woman who a was a popular athlete at a Christian University in Tennessee. She was suddenly afflicted with an illness, which was subsequently diagnosed as bacterial meningitis. The entire university—students and faculty— established a prayer vigil, asking students to pray for the stricken student's healing, in ten-minute segments, around the clock. Because of their faith, and the intensity of their prayers, they were convinced she would be fully healed. As matters worked out, the meningitis invaded her blood stream, and damaged tissue to the extent that both of her legs had to be amputated to save her life. According to the article many of the students were disillusioned that she was not fully healed, because of the clear statements of scripture, "Ask, and it shall be given you." And "All things are possible to him who believes." They began to question their faith and asked questions such as: "Does prayer really work?" "Why was she not healed with so many praying for her?" "Does God respond to prayer?" The article concluded that the experience made many students search for a deeper meaning to their faith.

Difficult times test our resolve and our faith. It is important that when these times do come—that we are grounded in what scripture really promises. And it doesn't promise that life will be without trials— if we believe. To the contrary, it tells us that the rain and sun fall on the faithful and the faithless. But it also tells us that whatever befalls us that there is help, and there can be peace with our trials—beyond understanding, even when there isn't understanding of our circumstances. Jesus of Nazareth faced these issues in the Garden of Gethsemane when He said, "My Soul is deeply grieved, to the point of death" and then prayed, "My Father, if it is possible, let this cup pass from me, yet not as I will, but as Thou will." (Matthew 26: 38,39)

"When Life Seems Unfair" deals with the question of the fundamental fairness and justice of life as it is played out. We have to conclude that while justice or fairness, as we see it, doesn't always win out —on a day-to day basis. God does not always pay off on Saturday night, but the One who created the universe does have an eternal plan, and that plan will prevail in the reaches of His time. Our task is to try to work within that plan, as we have the wisdom to see it, on a daily basis. And a part of that is "taking up our cross" daily, whatever that cross may be, and following Him.

When Life Seems Unfair

There are times in our life, when it just seems "it ain't fair"
When the bad guys win, the good guys lose, when the bulls,
        are run over by the bears.
Our sense of justice is offended, somehow it doesn't seem right
That there are times when one's benevolent efforts are rewarded
        with a pitiful plight.

For if we read specific scriptures, things seem abundantly clear:
"Pray without ceasing" "Ask and it shall be given,"
        all music to our ears
"All things are possible" "God answers prayer," so it says, too
So it would seem that His faithful, would have protection from
        disaster's milieu.

But scripture also says "The sun and the rain fall equally on the
        righteous and the wrong."
The Master said, "Take up your cross and follow me" on
        life's path long.
And "You must give up your life to find it" a paradox it seems
So when the storms of life come, we wrestle with what it all means.

We ask why is the undeserved one healed, when the righteous
        one is not?
Why does the faithless one walk, while the faithful lies
        in his burial plot?
It is in those difficult times, beyond our comprehension,
        and pious platitudes ring hollow
When we have sought to serve Him and others well,
        yet in our grief we wallow.

In candor we don't always have the answer as to the how
        and the why
Nor will you find a rational explanation from your pastor,
        priest or rabbi.
So, what can we say, when the heavy rains, into our life come
When the pain and hurt reach the depths of our soul,
        and our feelings numbed.

Beginning in the beginning, God creates, and gives us the
        freedom of many choices.
And the choices we make often affect not only us, but others who
        have had no voice.
Sometimes by the choices we make, we bring on our own woes
At other times, things happen in our lives, for reasons,
        only God knows.

At times, and in some events we're certain that God intervenes
To take us out of harms way, for reasons we are unable to glean.
Yet we're thankful for deliverance that has come to us
And are quick to give Him credit, when we discuss.

If it's true then, that in each our lives, there will be both
        plenty and drought,
We need to understand, that while He knows us and our lives,
        inside and out.
That the trials of our life are times of testing and times of growth
Even though, if we had our choice, we'd choose another loaf.

So what is it then, that those who walk in faith have,
        that others do not
It is the assurance that God is love, will prevail in His time,
        whatever life has wrought.
That what happens in our life is important, a golden thread
        in the tapestry of God's plan,
And by our attitudes and choices, we can make change,
        for good, in our life limited span.

It is the knowledge that whatever comes in our days,
    God will be with us through it all
To give us courage to cope, wisdom's vision, hope for the future,
    from winter to fall.
That while we will not always have answers each day,
    as to the how and the why
He Loves us, gives peace, has a plan for us, in all things,
    Ultimate control, will edify.

Scriptural references: Psalm 73,
Matthew 5:45, 7:7; Mark 9:23,
Luke 9:23–25, 1 James 2

The Last Visit

As Solomon so wisely observes in Ecclesiastes, there is a time to be born and a time to die. We celebrate birth, but we swing between uncomfortable and grief at death. While we like to celebrate the life lived of a loved one, we grieve over the loss of their presence. The last year has been a difficult one for me personally, losing my mother and brother to death, and losing three very close friends, each of whom died. I spent many hours with two of those friends, watching them die slowly. I would not trade anything for those hours with those two friends, but it was a difficult time. One wrestles with what to say, and not say. My dialogues with both of them ran similar courses. One, I went into with no hesitance, the other I wasn't sure what was "right." In both situations, I asked for help beyond myself. I have no doubt that I received direction, because I know I would not have had the courage to pose some of the questions I asked, nor the wisdom to answer some of the questions asked of me. They were not my questions, nor my answers. In each case, I am glad that I went to see them, even though it was difficult. And, I was glad to learn again, that help is there, if we will but ask. If I were asked to go again, I'd go in a heartbeat.

The Last Visit

She called and asked if I could come again
To visit my friend, her husband, to help his spirits mend.
It's so difficult, this hulk of a man, my friend since a child
The sickness he has, and its treatments, have his body defiled.

I had gone several times before, we'd talk old times
Talked about sports, about girlfriends, and our special lines.
We'd enjoyed and relived those exaggerated memories of our past
Time and life since then, had been on fast forward, gone way too fast.

What would I talk about this time, for he was barely able to speak?
It was torment for me, to see his pain, he, so drawn and weak.
I knew, though, I must go again, and again, to his last day
But since I must do all of the talking, what would I say?

I asked God for help, that I might speak the right words
To encourage him, give him hope, before he fell to this scourge.
As I sat in his living room, he on his couch, just he and I alone
There was Another with us, giving me thoughts and words,
        not my own.

I told him, he, like I, had been far from perfect through his life
But, that he, as I, had done the best he could, for his children
        and wife
I talked about the qualities of his life that I most admired
His qualities of integrity, loyalty to friends, industry, his love,
        how they inspired.

I asked if he had made peace with those he had fought.
"Yes, but there are some. . . " "Let it go now," I said, so it would
        account for naught.
Then I told him that, he was at the beginning of a new adventure
There'd be no more pain of this world, though a lot of things about it,
        we weren't sure.

"But we do know, and the promise is, that each of us, in our time,
    will take that journey.
We shall get up and walk, and throw away our life's disabilities
    and the hospital's gurney.
And for those who had sought, though often failed,
    to serve or help others.
There will come a time, when we shall all be together,
    living as brothers."

So though it was time, for him, on his journey to depart
I, and all those whom he'd loved, we'll be coming along,
    he just had a head start.
And then, I held his hands in mine, and asked God to take him
    safely home
I thanked Jesus for his forgiveness and grace, the promise that
    He would not leave us alone.

Though I know not what future the next moment of life holds for me
And though I know not what lies ahead, in that new life,
    beyond the sea.
Yet, I know that whatever it is, I look forward with anticipation,
    not with fear.
For I know, I shall see my Lord, my old friend,
    and those I have loved, and held so dear.

Ten Commandments of Marriage

"Ten Commandments of Marriage" was written twenty-five years ago when I taught a young adult couples' class. I gave a copy of the commandments to each couple. I don't know that it helped all of them, but for the most part, they are still together. It is written in Old English, the language of the King James' version of the Bible. Some years later, before each of my two children, Andy and Sandy, were married, I required that each of them and their spouses go to dinner with Ellen and me. As a condition of the dinner, before we ate, each couple had to suffer what I called my "Pre-Dinna" lecture. Following my talk, I gave each of them a printed copy of "Ten Commandments of Marriage." Both couples have it framed in their homes. After more than two decades of marriage for each, they are both still together and happily, despite the stress of raising three teenage children apiece. I am thankful each day for my children and their spouses, Carolyn and Carl, and pray for them daily as partners and parents.

"The Ten Commandments of Marriage" includes practical suggestions: Love, a lot of Patience, a lot of commitment, a strong Faith, a willingness to Listen more than you talk, a willingness to Accept each other for who you are, a willingness to Change when change is needed, and a pinch of Luck for good measure.

Ten Commandments of Marriage

1. Thou shalt love thy spouse with all thy heart and soul—even to the ends of the earth, but thou shalt respect and preserve thy spouse as the special and unique person he is, even as thyself. (cf. Ephesians 5:22–31)

2. It has been said that man shall leave his father and mother and cleave until his wife. Thou shalt put thy wife before all the world, before thyself, thy mother and father, thy friend and neighbor—yes, even thy children. (cf. Genesis 2:24)

3. Thou shalt communicate and share with thy spouse every day of thy life through all the senses, speaking, listening, touching, seeing with understanding, and thou shalt be slow to speak, quick to listen, and slow to anger, for anger shall lead you to wrong; and do not let the sun set on your anger lest it grow within and consume you. (cf. James 1:9)

4. Thou shalt not set thy goals on material things, neither money, nor status, nor power, nor control, but thou shalt set thy life's purpose on those eternal yet intangible things such as love, sharing, caring, and purposeful life, for what profiteth a man or woman if he gains the whole world but has not eternal conviction of life purpose. (cf. Psalm 49; Matthew 16: 25-16)

5. Thou shalt forgive and forget with a full heart, and thy family shall call thee blessed; and thou shalt love thy spouse for what he is and forgive him for what he is not. (cf. Matthew 5:7)

6. Thou shalt always remember that thy body, which has been given to you, is the Temple of the Holy Spirit and you shalt therefore neither defile thy body nor mind with excessive food, nor drink, nor any foreign substance, but thou shalt preserve thy body and the endowment given to you to the best of thy ability. (cf. 1st Corinthians 6:17)

7. Consider the lilies of the field and thou shalt not unduly worry about the future, for today has enough problems to occupy thy hours, for thy worry adds nothing to the solution of your problems, is a burden to thy spouse and accomplishes nothing.
(cf. Matthew 6:27, 34)

8. Cleanliness is next to Godliness, and thou shalt render all reasonable assistance to maintain an orderly home, a clean body and mind, and a neat attire. (cf. John Wesley)

9. This above all, to thine ownself and thy spouse be truthful and true for thou should be the best friend that he shall ever have.
(cf. John 8:32)

10. Together—Honor the Lord thy God who will release the bonds of fear and set you free; Let Him and His truth be the master of the household, and thy children shall rise up and call thee Blessed.
(cf. Exodus 20: 2–3)

Part Two
Personal Reflections

My Absolute Best

"How do I love thee? Let me count the ways. / I love thee to the depth and breadth and height / My soul can reach when falling out of sight." So Elizabeth Barrett Browning expressed her love for her husband Robert Browning in *Sonnets from the Portuguese*. Would that I had such beautiful words to express the depth of my love for my beloved Ellen. But words are a gift and my gift is limited. I've thought about it many times and tried to express to her how I felt, and I concluded that simpler is better. My love is simply my absolute best! My best friend, my best lover, my best counselor, my best homemaker, my best advisor, my best critic, my best nurse when I am ill, my best encourager when I am down, my best equalizer when I am up, but above all, I know that she loves me best, unconditionally, without reservation, without ceasing—she is simply my best everything.

For this type of love I am eternally grateful and undeservedly blessed. She is, simply stated, *my absolute best!*

My Absolute Best

When I first saw her, it didn't take long, I quickly knew
I was attracted by her smile, her grace, and her loveliness, too
I knew immediately, she was, for me, different than all the rest
But not in my wildest dreams, did I know,
        she would become my absolute best.

For a time, I was cautious, thought, should I really dare?
The more we're together, I knew she's the one, I would care.
I had never known anyone before, quite like her
She put my head in a tizzy, my heart in a stir.

Our marriage was the happiest day of my life, 'til then
I knew there'd be no other, no matter where or when.
From that day forward, she has always put me above all, first
Sought to love me, care for me, satisfy my every want and thirst.

And if I were to search for another like her, all of my life
I could never find another to compare, with my loving wife.
She is my best friend, my best lover, my best support
She is my best nurse in sickness, my best protector of our homeport.

She is my best admirer, my best advisor, my best defender.
She is my best provider in need, and my best heart's mender.
She is my best counselor, when my soul's distressed.
She is my absolute everything, in all of my being,
        she is my absolute best.

Children Through Grandparents' Eyes

You've seen the bumper stickers that read: LET ME TELL YOU ABOUT MY GRANDCHILDREN. We all have said, "So what!" Now I know differently! I have six grandchildren from ages twelve to twenty-one, and wow are they great! Grandchildren prompted someone to say, "If I'd known grandchildren were so much fun, I would have had them first." I won't ask you to let me tell you about each one, but collectively, they are the joy of my life, as are my children and my wife. But we do tend to look at our grandchildren differently than our children, maybe because we can just love them, and don't have to take care of them. And, as I found with my own children, grandchildren always behave much better for grandparents than they ever do for their parents. Anyway, mine are very, very special, as I am sure you feel yours are.

Children Through Grandparents' Eyes

God gives us children mercifully, when we are young
For age saps our energy, strength, and patience,
     when our spring is sprung.
But age does not steal the loving memories and times we've had
With our dear children, working through, with them, the good times
     and bad.

Yet one of the greatest joys that I have ever known
Is to watch the growth of grandchildren,
     as they seek to strive on their own.
Without the pressure of the daily grind.
A grandparent's love is complete, and often blind.

All we see are those growing little ones, so bright and so dear
Their unlimited futures, how they love us, and we them revere.
Though deep inside, we know they're not as perfect as we would say,
But then, we don't have to deal with their parents'
     travails of every day.

We feel quite comfortable with all of this, you know,
Because we had our time in the trenches, wrestling with children's
     ebb and flow.
We know, too, that our children must deal with concerns,
     we never saw,
A different society they face, with so many things ugly and raw.

So we give thanks for the joys and love each of our children
     and grandchildren bring.
And likewise, have compassion for their parents,
     who must worry about many things.
We pray that each might have the wisdom
     and patience to face each day,
As they guide and direct our beloved grandchildren, along life's way.

And we pray that God might give us the judgment to think twice
Before we give too much unsolicited and ancient advice.
Though wisdom is supposed to come with age and experience,
      with ease
They can choose to listen, then make their best judgment,
      and do as they please.

To Granddaddy's House He'd Go

This poem is about my son's special relationship with his grandfather, which was grounded in their mutual enjoyment of old horror movies. Sometimes we have to stretch to find the point of bonding with two generations younger, but once the bridge has been found, the connection can be the glue of a lasting relationship. Such was the case with my son, Andy, and my father. Until the day of my dad's death, the two of them had a special friendship cemented by "horror" movies. Andy, thirty-five years later, still loves the old black and white "Dracula" (Bela Lugosi) and "Frankenstein" (Lon Chaney Jr.) movies.

To Granddaddy's House He'd Go

Around the corners, over the streets, and through the trees, he rode.
Andy adventured each Saturday to visit his Granddaddy,
    at his abode.
Lickety-split, as fast as he could peddle, on his purple banana bike
Riding like the wind, lest he meet Dracula or a ghost, he might.

For Andy, with Grandaddy, watched old monster movies,
    in the afternoon
And as his mind thought of Frankenstein, he couldn't arrive too soon.
Grandaddy's house was old and large,
    to him an ancient castle, it appeared.
But to see his Grandaddy, get cookies and Coke, always excited,
    as he drew near.

Grandaddy was always happily awaiting, he stood at the door,
    asked Andy to come in.
They'd sit down together, where the show was just beginning,
    in Grandaddy's den
Maybe "The Mummy," "The Abominable Snowman," "Dracula,"
    or "House of Frankenstein."
They watched, talked about many things, while Andy had visions of
    cookies in mind.

Grandaddy's kitchen refrig seemed miles away,
    always had a generous supply of Coke.
Grandaddy with a smile, would say, "Help yourself!"
    but to go alone, to Andy was no joke.
Then, Granddaddy, a twinkle in his eye, his arm around Andy,
    he'd say, "I'll go with you."
They'd each pick a cold bottle of Coke, grab a handful of peanuts,
    and cookies, too.

When the last werewolf had howled, with a full tummy and a smile,
      Andy'd say good-bye.
"Are you coming back next week?" Grandaddy asked.
      Andy'd say, "I'll sure try!"
He vowed he'd come back, though it took great courage,
      with all those scary old things
'Cause he loved his Grandaddy, the Cokes, cookies, even the frightful
      ghouls, with wings.

If Sandy Should Call

The story related in "If Sandy Should Call" is true, even the part about the honeymoon with our daughter and son-in-law. We have been married forty-six years and they have been married twenty. I wrote this for their anniversary. Actually, the open-door-open-ear policy applied to all three of our children. They were all the same. If we heard a call in the night, when they called, "Mom," we knew they felt sick. If they were frightened, they called for "Mom and Dad." In the sense of wanting to "be there" for our children—if they should call—I believe it is universal for parents. Regardless of our age, they are still our children. Before my mother died in 1998 at age ninety-one, she still called me, at age sixty-seven, her "baby."

Years ago in my law practice, I had an elderly client come to my office one day. I knew she was elderly, but the better part of wisdom says you don't ask a woman her age. She was upset, and said she was going to Miami that day to take care of her son. His wife had just left him, and he was recovering from open-heart surgery. Thinking he might be forty or forty-five, I asked "How old is your son?" She replied "Seventy-two." I said, "It ain't over 'til it's over is it? Our job as parents is never over until our last breath, is it?" She agreed. So parenting is a lifetime responsibility. But I would give up everything I own rather than to have missed it.

If Sandy Should Call

Our new baby girl was born on New Year's Eve,
　　　so special and petite, so small.
She slept in an old worn crib, used by her brothers,
　　　right next to us, bunting and all.
We wanted her close by us, so on her we could keep a close eye
Could hear her every breath, her every move, and could hear her cry.

When she was six months old, she moved to her own bright new room
But to her mom and dad, though, we knew it was right,
　　　but just a bit too soon.
From the day she moved in, we left our door open, for our little doll
To be sure that we could hear her in the night, if Sandy should call.

And when she was four, our door was still open, it was not just a fad
We wanted to comfort her, if sick, or had a bad dream,
　　　and call, "Mom and Dad."
Always listening, even as we slept, with one ear open,
　　　restful sleep was stalled
To be sure that we could hear her in the night, if Sandy should call.

When she was seven, about eight o'clock, we'd put her to bed
After we'd done our home work, and maybe a story we'd read
When bedtime came, she'd write notes to us, hoping to stall
Off to bed, much later for us, leave the door open,
　　　so if Sandy should call.

And when she became a teenager, doing all the things they do
It still was no different, each night before bed, she'd say, "I love you."
Maybe she'd had a bad day at school, she'd come in and tell all
Even then, the door was still open, so we could hear,
　　　if Sandy should call.

After high school, she still lived at home, had her own job
I couldn't close the door—opened a crack, as I turned the knob.
When she turned in at night, even then, she'd take to bed with her,
     an old lion rag doll
And of course, I'd leave our door open to hear, if Sandy should call.

Later, she married—that bittersweet day,
     when I gave my daughter away.
And with her fine husband, they invited both in-laws,
     at honeymoon house to stay
I'd never heard of such a thing, a honeymoon trip,
     with in-laws and all
Even then, I couldn't help it, left my door open a crack,
     so if Sandy should call.

The years have passed, her own family,
     and three lovely children, they have
They've now grown to teenagers, girlfriends,
     sports and atomic balm salve.
Though she's gone, I still keep the door open, phone by my bed,
     after all
I want to be there and hear her call, just in case,
     if Sandy should call.

And though it's been twenty years now that she's gone
With none rattling 'round the house, we go to bed much earlier,
     with a yawn.
I know that she, too, keeps her door open,
     so that she can hear her children call, one and all.
As for me, I'll always keep my door open, as long as I am here,
     just to hear, if Sandy should call.

The Corner and the Bump

Recently I had occasion to go for a leisurely walk where the home in which I was raised is located. It is on a large corner lot and a sidewalk traverses the entire block. As I walked on that old sidewalk where I had played more than sixty years ago, I came to a bump or break—the same one that was there when I was a child. The sight of it brought many fond memories of playtimes. It also brought the recollection that for a time in my young life, that the bump and the corner of my parents' lot at the other end, represented the full extent of my known world. I had been cautioned many times never to go beyond the corner and the bump, but never told why nor what lay beyond the edge of my world. All my inexperienced mind knew was that there were things unknown to fear "out there," and I must always stay between the corner and the bump where life was "safe." As I recalled those days and my thoughts, I wondered if, as adults, we too often stay in safe harbor, rather than take a chance, to go for it—even if we fail. Are you, like I was as a young lad, living your life between the corner and the bump? We'll never know what lies waiting for us in this world unless we take a chance and go beyond the corner and the bump.

The Corner and the Bump

When I turned four, I got a shining new tricycle, it was blue and
    white and red.
I rode it daily, up and down in front of our home, my bottom to its
    seat was wed.
But when I turned five my world expanded, I rode beyond the home-
    line stump
Though fearful, I'd go a bit farther, but no farther than from the
    corner to the bump.

The corner and the bump in the sidewalk, like the edge of my world
    that was flat.
I didn't dare go beyond the bump, I might fall off the edge
    and go ker-splat.
Besides there might be all kinds of scary things out there,
    I might get into a fight.
Who knows what might lie beyond the corner,
    maybe things that go bump in the night.

For a year, the corner and the bump were my world,
    I scarcely looked beyond
That was my domain, like the small fish,
    who lived his whole life in a small pond.
I saw other children, coming and going, making daily trips,
    on their merry way
Exploring new adventures, new ideas, new playmates,
    new worlds to survey.

So many people live their lifetime,
    without extending their world, reaching for the stars
Placing on themselves limitations, fearing failure,
    like living in a Mason jar.
Are you willing to take a chance, to try something new,
    to take a leap or a jump?
Or is your world like mine was, limited,
    and lived between the corner and the bump?

In Our Back Yard

As a young mother, my grandmother, Harriet McCoy Woolslair, wrote a poem bearing the same title, which appears in Part Three of this book. Her poem was published in 1931 in a national parent-teacher journal. When my mother died I found it among her papers. I remembered my mother's stories about her back yard in the early 1900s, in a wilderness village called Buckingham, Florida. In her backyard she saw alligators, snakes, panthers, bobcats, gopher turtles and other varmints. This poem is about my children's back yard a half-century later. Even in the city, not a lot had changed there.

In Our Back Yard

In our back yard, many years ago
A half-acre of green grass, each week we'd mow.
So the playground was ready, for the children to come
What a joy to hear the shrieks of little ones,
        daily playing, on the run.

In our back yard, many years ago
Our children played games, as o'er the years they'd grow.
Games of tag, football, hide and seek, race and chase
At hourly intervals, stop for a drink, with red and sweaty face.

In our back yard, many years ago
Children stood their turn, to swing the rope swing,
        bobbing to and fro.
It hung from a stately pine, standing tall in the air
Children often climbed the rope, hand by hand,
        with strength to spare.

In our back yard, many years ago
In springtime, a mysterious big-footed bunny,
        came at night, to quietly tiptoe,
Hiding brightly colored Easter eggs, to be hunted,
        some with coin, others, candy
And the one who found the most, earned a special prize,
        fine and dandy.

In our back yard, may years ago
There'd be lightning bugs at dusk, flying about with light aglow.
The children, so excited, would chase to catch them,
        in their little hands
Speak gently, magic words, pet them, send them in the air,
        off to distant lands.

In our back yard, many years ago
Many little creatures lived and played, along the banks,
     where the waters flow.
There were bunnies, 'possums,
     raccoons with blackpatch eyes, ducks and otters, too
Bushy-tailed squirrels, racing up and down the trees,
     nervously twitching, in a stew.

In our back yard, many years ago
Were large beautiful and stately trees, their lovely branches to show
Water oaks, pines, royal palms, poincianas,
     with blooms of purple and gold
Carved initials of boys and girls, special friends,
     around their girth were scrolled.

In our back yard, many years ago
Did nature a menagerie of gorgeous birds, bountifully on us bestow.
Mocking birds, cardinals, blue jays, woodpeckers, crows and robins
Fussed and sang alternately, and their beautiful melodies,
     began each day again.

In our back yard, many years ago
The fun, joy and laughter, all the children had,
     they'd one day outgrow.
But the treasured memories of those years, to each of us still flow
Of those times past, in our back yard, many years ago.

On Manuels Branch

In 1963, my wife, Ellen, and I moved with our young children to a home that backed up to a then navigable stream known as Manuels Branch. The branch was named for one of the early settlers to our area, Manuel Gonzales, who came to this country in 1886. Ellen and I still live there, now thirty seven years later. There has been a lot of living done on Manuels Branch, not only by our family, but by many others, including many generations before us. "On Manuels Branch" is a nostalgic poem about the wonderful experiences three generations of children of our family have had growing up on and playing on the banks of the branch.

On Manuels Branch

When I was a boy there was a creek near my home
Called Manuels Branch, often up and down its banks I'd roam.
It wound like a snake, under roads and trees for more than a mile
We hunted for "wild animals," tracked like Indians, all the while.

And, I'd fish its shallow waters for bass and crab and brim.
On a warm summer afternoon, we'd even go down for a swim.
Then I grew older, left home to begin my own new life
But often shared memories of the winding branch
        with my new young wife.

Years later I returned, we bought an old house on the flowing creek
My young children played up and down its banks,
        soldiers and hide and seek.
And, as I watched them play, I wondered if long years before we
        came
Young Indian boys played up and down the creek, just the same.

As my children grew older, they would gig gar, use cast nets and fish
Look for snakes and gators, swimming, then prohibited, only a wish.
They built tree houses, trenches, and army forts along the banks
Or maybe a bridge, built with castaway lumber as walking planks.

The tidal waters most times came in and out, ever so slow
But come summer rains, excitement, objects raced by,
        caught in the flow.
Rope swings strung from high branches,
        across the creek would swing
Games of Tarzan, Escape, rope-climbing, and romantic tales to bring.

They built boats and rafts to navigate, and homemade oars
And secret clubhouses along the banks, with palm frond doors.
An adventure trip up the creek, just a hundred yards or so
With visions of Huck Finn, Tom Sawyer, as the boat tilts to and fro.

And when they grew older, they walked the creek,
     with special friends
Telling tales of the earlier days, all the adventures,
     high waters and winds.
Then, one by one, they moved away,
     to make their own families and homes
But they would return to relive adventures,
     or just sit at their place of shalom.

Still later, as their own children came, and began to grow
The little ones would play along the same banks I played so long ago.
They wandered up and down the banks of the branch,
     now overgrown.
The very same spots, where now three generations' family
     adventures were sewn.

They fished the creek, cast nets, and gigged for the gars
And imagined pirates and monsters to attack, all from afar.
Now they too, are growing older, come to the branch less often
But I know they'll come back, to enjoy and remember when.

The enormous oaks, pines and palms,
     which have stood here since I was a lad
Have seen the many adventures, excitement,
     and fantasies, so many have had.
So, now in my twilight, as I sit here looking at this tired old creek
I wonder if I'll see a new generation of children, its mysteries to seek.

The Wooden Gravestone

The scheming plot of this family story is true, but Joseph Sheppard wasn't born in 1840, and he didn't die of diaper rash at the age of three. He never died because he was never born.

He was the figment of the imagination of my young son and his friend, Cary, who hatched a "sinister" plot to scare their sisters, Sandy and Anne. Unfortunately for the boys, the girls were more perceptive than they could have envisioned.

The Wooden Gravestone

Cary and Andy had sisters, Anne and Sandy by name.
They loved their sisters, but loved to frighten them, just the same.
One day on the banks of Manuels Branch, they conceived a plan
That was sure to scare them out of their wits, both Sandy and Anne.

Both Andy and Cary, worked for hours, conceiving
    and hatching the plot
To construct an "old" gravesite, of an ancient ancestor,
    believe it or not.
Aye, mate, 'twas Joseph Sheppard by name, the dead one would be
Born in eighteen and forty, died of diaper rash
    before the age of three.

They carefully crafted and printed the wooden gravestone
Even beneath the surface, they planted some fake plastic bones
Placed flowers 'round the site, near the branch's edge
Hung up a skull and crossbones, wrote out Joseph's heritage.

Then they asked Ann and Sandy to come out and play
Told them they'd made a frightful discovery, along the way
Said there was an old grave and bones, down by the creek
To dig up the bones of Joseph Sheppard, would be really neat.

When the girls came upon the gravestone, that awesome sight
They both laughed aloud, kicked it over, it's sham to expedite.
So, the carefully laid plans of terror, had gone up in smoke
The saga of Joseph Sheppard's fatal diaper rash,
    was on these two crafty boys, the joke.

The Little Green Boat

"The Little Green Boat" is yet another reflection of an earlier time, when children were young, and about their adventures on Manuels Branch in a green boat that served them well for years.

The Little Green Boat

In days gone by, a little green boat was docked at our creek
Not sure where we got it, but to our children it was just so, neat.
It was the vehicle for marvelous children's adventures and trips
Though it was beat up, and glued together, shoddy workmanship.

That beat up old tug was something special, to our little Sandy
Even though she had to share it with her brothers, Jay and Andy.
She and her friend Anne took frequent trips, even beyond the bridge
They had to venture beneath the road, and cross a sandbar ridge.

One day, after laying plans, on a marvelous fishing voyage they went
In preparing the boat, a tasty lunch, a whole morning was spent
But by the time they reached the river, both were very tired
For 'twas a hot summer day, and they'd both heavily perspired.

They caught nary a fish that day, but had loads of fun
Brought nothing back but smelly leftover bait, and a soggy bun.
Faces red, and sunburned, sweaty, but elated from their glorious day
But both too tired when they returned, to stay out and play.

And many times after that day, when time for nap or for bed
I'd rock my Sandy to sleep, telling her stories, imagined and read.
But the one she always loved best, her choice for me to tell
Were tales and sagas of the Little Green Boat, she knew so well.

Grandma's Book of Life

My wife, Ellen, is not only a wonderful wife, chief cook and bottlewasher, along with many other titles, but also a mother and "grandma." We have been blessed to have each of our six grandchildren live nearby, so that we have been able to watch them grow up—almost day by day. Ellen has always been a veritable storehouse of practical wisdom, and imparts that wisdom to the grandchildren, freely, and on a regular basis. One of our grandchildren, now in his late teens, began to kid Grandma a bit about her statements and affirmations about life and how to behave. After hearing one of her stories, he jokes, "Now that statement is found on page 65 of "Grandma's Book of Life." I only wish that she had or we could write down these pearls of wisdom that she has given to the grandchildren over the years. Maybe that will be the next volume. It should sell a million copies.

Grandma's Book of Life

She's a wonderful lady, our grandma, and oh so wise
In good old common sense, she'd win the prize.
She's always willing to give her sage advice
From "Grandma's Book of Life," that wisdom without price.

Always be thoughtful, in all the things you do.
Always be truthful, it will pay rich dividends for you.
Always respect your parents, because they've loved you so.
They have given so much of themselves, more than you know.

And always give it the very best that you can
Whether it be in school, in sports, in life, or the race you ran.
And even though you won't always win the race
Give to it all that you have, in whatever test you face.

Prepare each day for the worst, but expect the best
And approach each task, with confidence, with fervor and zest.
And in whatever you do, be precise in how you measure
For then you will find, what you produce will be a treasure.

And, take time to enjoy, as life passes through
Else you may miss so much of living, important to you.
Always keep your sense of humor, at yourself even laugh
For even in your successes, will be many mistakes, many a gaff.

And, when you love, be certain the one you select
Is the one to live your life with, and not easily cast off or reject
Be happy with who you are, and with the talents you are given
For, 'tis the unhappy person, trying to be who he isn't,
        his efforts misdriven.

When I look back over all the things the children have been taught
Lessons in life, no book could teach, nor at any price be bought
I shall never forget that unwritten book—"Grandma's Book of Life."
For she and her book have prepared our grandchildren
        for so many of life's joys and strife.

The Tickle Box

My uncle, John K. Woolslair Jr, was born in 1908, and lived and grew up in a rural community—then cow country known as Buckingham, Florida. At the age of six, Uncle John contracted infantile paralysis, which was later called polio. From it, he received a severely withered leg. There were no cures, no Salk vaccine, and no accepted treatments for polio in those days, other than several treatment methods developed by Sister Kenney. Part of that treatment was electrical stimulation. Electrical currents were placed on his young leg, and to him it tickled each time. My grandmother would give him "tickle box" treatments three times daily. His three older sisters would gather in the room to watch, and as soon as the treatment started, my Uncle John would begin to laugh, and all three girls, as well as grandmother would laugh with him. Even this illness and disability through the tickle box, became a "fun" thing for him, as well as giving the whole family at least three good laughs each day. John Woolslair carried that joyous, happy attitude as well as and in spite of his withered leg, with him the rest of his life. He was a courageous man and never thought of or treated his disability as such, but simply as a minor inconvenience. When he was in high school, he tried out for and made the school football team. Even though he was small in stature, the coach placed him at the guard position, lining up next to the center, because there he did not have to run, but simply block. He was an inspiration to his teammates and school, just for being there. Later, as World War II broke out, Uncle John (then in his mid-thirties) enlisted in the Army, and went to Camp Blanding, Florida, where he took his physical examination. Needless to say, he did not pass the examination and was disappointed he could not serve. He enjoyed life to the end, even with his disability, and in his zest for life he was an inspiration to all who knew him. Would that we all had a tickle box that we might enjoy life, even the tough challenges, more.

The Tickle Box

My Uncle John Woolslair was a gregarious and jovial man
He was a friend of many, always ready to extend a hand.
As a prosecutor, he convicted those who committed crimes,
    mostly men.
As a lawman, his fairness was legion,
    even the felons became his friend.

Uncle John inspired many, as he limped through life,
    puffing his cigar.
He never considered his a disability,
    but an opportunity, life was his lodestar.
For you see, he was crippled, in 1914, when he was a lad,
    six years young
He contracted a disease, now called polio,
    withered his leg, but no iron lung.

My grandmother treated him, with the only remedies
    that they then knew
Proscribed by Sister Kenney, deep massage and aromatics,
    to name a few
But the one he liked best, the daily electric stimulation
    of his withered limb
Called it his "Tickle Box," 'cause it made him laugh,
    and made others laugh with him.

I've often wondered if that little box that made him laugh every day
Taught him to laugh at his problems, and enjoy life along the way
Whatever it was, he took each day as a gift,
    all life was good, he found.
Would that we each might have a tickle box,
    to give our life his joyous ground.

More Puppies

This day is about a glorious fun-filled day I recall many years ago, when my good friend and partner, Jay Brett, brought his two young children to our home to visit. Our seventy-pound Old English sheepdog had just given birth to eight puppies. The children did not know it when they came in. The poem is about their glee, as they were introduced to eight new puppies—two at a time.

More Puppies

Katie, Brian and their dad came to visit us one day
Their dad sat down, they sat on the floor, with toys to play.
I asked them if they had a little puppy, a dog or a cat
"No, neither one," they said, "no room at home for all of that."

Now, we had a wonderful Old English, named Maggie the Great
Who'd just had a litter of puppies, by number they were eight
What a busy mom she had been, feeding the cotton-balled litter
Their jumping, nipping and barking kept her all in a dither.

I asked Katie and Brian, if they'd like to see a couple of pups.
"Oh, yes," they said, their eyes aglitter as they leaped up.
So I brought two of the little ones from the washroom where they lay
Mother Maggie was so happy, to have a brief respite, a slight delay.

The children squealed and screamed with utter delight.
I asked if they'd like to see more puppies, "Oh, yes! All right!"
So two more cotton-ball pups, I brought in for them to see
They jumped up and down with uncontrolled glee.

Then I brought in two more, so now there were six.
"More puppies," they yelled, as they rolled among the mix.
"Would you like even more puppies?" I asked them out straight
"More puppies, more puppies," and now there were eight.

I said, "That's it, no more, that's all we have here."
"Oh thank you, thank you, we love each of the little dears."
There were eight fuzzy puppies, two little children, rolling around
Puppies yipping and licking, children squealing,
        what a wondrous sound.

I shall never forget Katie and Brian's uncontrollable laughter
Their shrieks of joy rang in my ears, for many weeks after.
What a wonderful time the children and eight puppies had that day
If only we big people could capture the joys of little children,
        along the way.

The John B.

I have a grandson named "John B." He's no better nor any worse than all of my six grandchildren. After all, they all are perfect in grandpa's eyes. John B.'s real name is John Vincent Barraco. When he was young he couldn't pronounce Vincent, so he gave his name as John Bencent Barraco. Hence I've always called him John B. And then there was the song about the sloop *John B.* John B. plays ice hockey. I was watching one of his games one evening and the words of "The John B." came to mind.

The John B.

My grandson, the John B., is very close to me
At twelve, he's one big muscle, as you can see.
His stomach looks like a large lamb's rack
Some call it washboard, some a six-pack.
He plays hockey, skates swiftly, checks them hard
Especially the boys with a bit of extra lard.
He moves away quickly, with neither pride nor guile,
Looks back at the fallen warrior, with a toothless smile.

Part Three
Reflections of My Heritage

Harriet McCoy Woolslair

My grandmother, Harriet McCoy, was born in Lima, Ohio, on September 13, 1879. Her future husband, John Kneeland Woolslair, moved to Fort Myers, Florida, from Beaver, Pennsylvania, in 1898, for health reasons. He had severe asthma attacks, and was told by doctors that if he was to survive an early death he must move to either Arizona or Florida. Concluding that Arizona was still wilderness—"Indian country,"—and not even a part of the United States until 1912, John Woolslair chose Florida. His mother had vacationed in Fort Myers, Florida, during the winter of 1896, staying at the Royal Palm Hotel for the winter, and felt Fort Myers (at least the Royal Palm Hotel) was quite nice. John Woolslair came to Fort Myers and found a thirty-acre site on the Orange River, which was a tributary of the Caloosahatchee River, in a rural community known as Buckingham. Although John's background was engineering, he surmised that he could put an orange grove on the thirty acres, and also grow pineapple, shipping his fruit by steamer to the north. In 1899 he visited relatives in Chillicothe, Ohio, and there met young Harriet McCoy, who had just graduated from college with a degree in English and literature. She planned to teach school.

Following an extended courtship, Harriet and John were married in 1903. John brought his new young bride to the "wilds" of Florida, though he had told her it was quite civilized. The only transportation to town from Buckingham was by boat. This first week there, John brought his bride to town on Saturday to shop for the month and for dinner. He told her that because the south side of First Street was where the saloons and livery stables were, the "ladies" should always stay on the north side where the dry good store and restaurant were located. Following her shopping for the coming weeks, they had a meal at the only restaurant. When they came out they spotted two men arguing on the "bad" side of the street. Suddenly, one drew his pistol from its holster, shot and killed his antagonist. Harriet was convinced she had made a mistake in moving to Florida.

In the five years that followed, beginning in 1904, Harriet bore four children, Elizabeth, Eleanor, Mary, and John Jr. Since there was no hospital nor medical care in Fort Myers, Harriet, the city girl, traveled back to Beaver by train each summer to have her children, and returned in the fall. Some poems in this volume were written by Harriet Woolslair when her children were young, several to my mother, Mary, when she was young, married and had her first child, my sister, while others were written after John died from a heart attack, complicated by his asthma in 1926. They express her feelings of grief, loss and faith.

Though she was only forty-seven when my grandfather died, she never remarried, and chose to live alone with her memories and her love lost until her death at eight-three.

I am grateful for the example, which my grandmother set for me—an example of integrity, of courage, and an abiding faith and commitment to her Lord and Savior, Jesus Christ. I did not realize until long after her death, the impact that the memory of her life would have on my life.

Courage Is My Shield

Courage is my shield,
I hold it close to me these darkened days
It does not stop the blows,
But they do not reach me,
Long ago I fashioned it,
Of faith and hope and prayer
Firmly bound. I know now
One must make his own shield.

To Mary, on Her Twenty-first Birthday

Twenty-one! A wife and mother
Brown-eyed baby of my girls.
Just a jiffy since I held you
Tired of play, with tousled curls.

Spanked you some when you were willful
Scolded you when you were "bad"—
Played with you when you were lonely
Loved you always—Mother—Dad.

So this birthday wish I send to you
All your years may happy be,
And the little daughter bring you
All that you have brought to me.

A Mother's Prayer at Noon

Dear Lord, the day is long and I am tired
I kneel to ask thy help along the way.
I have travelled far since early dawn
And must go on until the end of day.
So many little things have fretted me
They might have made my judgment err.
May love for them help many blind mistakes
I care so much—Lord, hear my prayer.

Lines to Daughter

When you were naughty, I spanked you
I wanted you to be good.
But when you spank your daughter
I do not think you should.

Mother Thoughts

Often as she walks she needs me—little toddler by my side.
Baby feet will strangely falter—baby steps might need a guide—
Paths are rough and might be lonely—often tread on marsh or stone.
"Heavenly Father," help me teach her—how to walk aright alone.

Still she needs me near for counsel, growing school girl straight
      and tall
Sums are hard—life's lessons harder, I'll be near if she should call
Things worth while she might pass over, in this glittering gay today-
"Heavenly Father," help me show her, better things along the way.

Life and love are beckoning onward, she will hurry on her way.
But as when we walked together, prayer for her at close of day.
Always in my thoughts I'll follow—tho her path leads far from me
Father,—guide her, bless her, keep her—little girl that used to be.

In Our Back Yard

In our back yard
The grass is scarce and brown
And flowers cannot raise their petaled heads.
For children play there all day long
And pick bouquets for Mother—pink and red.
The baby's washing flutters on the line
And swings of creaking rope that come and go
Resound with girlish laughter, boyish shouts—
In our back yard
So long ago.

In our back yard
The grass is thick and green
The lovely plants grow tall with perfect flowers.
The birds have found their shallow bath,
The stately sundial tells the shining hours.
But when I look on it I do not see
The chiseled stone, or posies growing in a row.
I only see my children at their play—
In our back yard
So long ago.

Afterthought

I cannot thank thee, Lord
For blessings and for joys of other years
For they are gone
The way is lonely now
I long for echoes of his voice
Await the firm, swift step
Of him I love.

But as I wait, thoughts come
Of love and peace and home.
Deep within my lonely heart
I feel the joys that have been mine.
So perfect, fear have felt this magic thrill
I bow my head in shame, I didn't thank thee then
For all those memories past, I now thank thee, Lord.

The Better Way

In God's plan, it might have been
That you, instead of me
Should walk the sunset trail alone
While days and months pass endlessly
The years are long to you with Him
It is but as a day
Because I love you, I am sure
This is the better way.

Christ at the Door

I opened the door of my heart
And Christ has come in to stay.
There are no shadows nor darkness
With the light of Eternal Day.
Now I go my way securely
For I feel His presence fair
And life has a richer meaning
Since I found Him waiting there.

Not Alone

The full moon flooded my garden
I was alone with memories dear.
A leaf stirred in the evening silence
The one I loved seemed near.
I felt God there in that silver gleam
And the one I loved with Him.
Some night from that moonlit garden,
I will walk away with them.

Light for the Lonely Road

To one in sorrow
I, too, have traveled this lonely road.
The way was dark and drear
I faltered and stumbled and plodded along
Forgetting that God was near.
But as I lingered in the gloom and found His Hand
And now He guides my way.
The road is not lonely, nor rough, nor dark
With the light of eternal day.

Sunset

In the span of years, God gave me my day
The afternoon sun is low in the west.
The hours are passing, and I need to test
My plans and time the way
I may use the hours of my closing day.
I will vision it now and do my best,
As sun sinks low in the golden west
Lighting my hours with the sunset ray.

I will be more thoughtful and always kind,
Making the best of what may be;
A thankful heart for heavenly care,
A helping hand a tolerant mind.
There still are hours that belong to me,
Shadows grow long, but the sky is fair.

Mary Woolslair Sheppard

My mother, Mary Woolslair Sheppard, was born July 29, 1907, in Beaver, Pennsylvania. I think she always resented her birthplace a bit, that she wasn't born in Fort Myers, Florida, where she lived all of her life. Her mother, Harriet Woolslair, engaged in early family planning. By that I mean she "arranged" for all of her children to be born in the summer months (July and August). The reason—the orange crop from the orange grove my grandfather owned on Orange River, would have been harvested, and she could take the train back to Beaver, Pennsylvania, where there were doctors and medical facilities. Harriet went back four summers to have four children in five years, returning in the fall with her newest family addition. Mary was the third.

My mother's full-time job was wife, mother, grandmother, and great grandmother. She left to her children and descendants a rich heritage and legacy of faith, love, loyalty, strength of character and wisdom.

When my mother died in her sleep in August 1998 I found only one writing among her papers that was in her handwriting, "On Stormy Days." She had many stormy days, when her father died when she was nineteen, when my sister died at forty-two, when my father died in 1971, when two of her grandsons died, and finally when her son, my brother, died in July 1998. I believe that this last storm was her end, for she died just a month later. To her last day, she maintained her positive, independent attitude, always seeking to find the good in others, and an unshakable faith in her Lord and her Savior, Jesus Christ. "On Stormy Days" speaks what she believed and how she lived through good and difficult times alike. I am grateful for the example she set, the way she lived her life, as well as the way she left this life.

On Stormy Days

When you cannot see the way,
When storm clouds fill the air,
It helps the worries, dear,
To know that God is there.

He is there waiting
Within ourselves we know.
He will guide our steps aright
As He onward bids us go.

When you need someone to help
When nothing is left for you.
In God's good hand, will He hold.
The strength to help you through.

Index

A Game of Cards 93

A Mother's Prayer at Noon (Harriet Woolslair) 153

A Prayer of Thanksgiving 62

Afterthought (Harriet Woolslair) 157

Better Way, The (Harriet Woolslair) 158

Blessing, The 17

Blessings Come Forth 43

Children Through Grandparents' Eyes 117

Christ at the Door (Harriet Woolslair) 159

Corner and the Bump, The 126

Courage Is My Shield (Harriet Woolslair) 151

Demands on Man, The 64

Eagle Has Landed, The 22

Eye of the Beholder, The 90

Forgive and Let Go 29

Grandma's Book of Life 138

Greatest Gift, The 75

If Sandy Should Call 123

In Our Back Yard (Harriet Woolslair) 156

In Our Back Yard 128

In Praise of Working Mothers 99

It's Time—To Fast 82

John B., The 145

Just Like My Dad 84

Last Visit, The 107
Learning to Laugh 73
Light for the Lonely Road (Harriet Woolslair) 161
Like a Two-edged Sword 7
Little Green Boat, The 136
Lines to Daughter (Harriet Woolslair) 154
Listen 52
Manly Tears 34
Money 67
More Puppies 142
Mother Thoughts (Harriet Woolslair) 155
My Absolute Best 115
My Advocate 3
Not Alone (Harriet Woolslair) 160
On Manuels Branch 131
On Stormy Days (Mary Woolslair Sheppard) 164
Pearls of Life 25
Prophets Without Honor 49
River of No Return, The 40
Sometimes 78
Sunset (Harriet Woolslair) 162
Ten Commandments of Marriage 110
Tickle Box, The 140
Times of Our Life, The 10
Through Children's Eyes 46
To Be or Not To Be 70
To Granddaddy's House He'd Go 120
To Mary, on Her Twenty-first Birthday (Harriet Woolslair) ... 152
Tomorrow 80
Unto the Least of Them 60

Waiting	55
Wave, The	32
What Price	58
When Life Seems Unfair	102
Who is This Man	87
Why Questions of Life, The	13
Why 2 K	37
Wooden Gravestone, The	134
Worry–Let It Be	96

Printed in the United States
19076LVS00006B/1-81